LEARNING
WITH OTHERS

LEARNING
WITH OTHERS

*Collaboration as a Pathway
to College Student Success*

CLIFTON CONRAD
and TODD LUNDBERG

JOHNS HOPKINS UNIVERSITY PRESS
Baltimore

© 2022 Johns Hopkins University Press
All rights reserved. Published 2022
Printed in the United States of America on acid-free paper
2 4 6 8 9 7 5 3 1

Johns Hopkins University Press
2715 North Charles Street
Baltimore, Maryland 21218-4363
www.press.jhu.edu

Library of Congress Cataloging-in-Publication Data

Names: Conrad, Clifton, author. | Lundberg, Todd, author.
Title: Learning with others : collaboration as a pathway to college student
success / Clifton Conrad and Todd Lundberg.
Description: Baltimore : Johns Hopkins University Press, 2022. | Includes
bibliographical references and index.
Identifiers: LCCN 2021022737 | ISBN 9781421443515 (hardcover) |
ISBN 9781421443522 (ebook)
Subjects: LCSH: Education, Higher—Aims and objectives—United States. |
Academic achievement—United States.
Classification: LCC LA227.4 .C663 2022 | DDC 378.73—dc23
LC record available at https://lccn.loc.gov/2021022737

A catalog record for this book is available from the British Library.

*Special discounts are available for bulk purchases of this book. For more information,
please contact Special Sales at specialsales@jh.edu.*

CONTENTS

ACKNOWLEDGMENTS

We owe this book to collaborative learning—to learning with, from, and for others about what makes for student success in college. The project now spans nearly a decade. Across that time, we have engaged one another and scores of others in ongoing dialogue, moving to an alternative vision of undergraduate education for a diverse democracy and the educational practices that need to be incorporated across our nation's colleges and universities.

In more ways than we can count, this project belongs to other people who were, in so many ways, already aware of what we were writing up. Foremost are students and teachers at Minority-Serving Institutions (MSIs) that we visited during a national study of programs and practices at twelve MSIs. The study itself would not have been possible without the energy, insight, and commitment of Marybeth Gasman. She co-orchestrated the study and data analysis and co-wrote a book on our findings with me (Clif).

Mainstream higher education seemed to ask the study participants, a student at the College of Menominee Nation mused, to work "twice as hard." Yet they sat with us—white researchers from a predominantly white institution with a history of selectivity and exclusion—to share stories about what educational success looked like to them, how they were finding ways to be successful in college in their own eyes, and how they were hacking undergraduate education to make space for their success. We are indebted to them for their time, their stories, and their patience. We got more far more than we gave. To this day, continuing to read again through stories fixed in interview transcripts we see again the faces of people who wanted college to serve those coming to their MSIs. We were welcomed to "our college" by learners and teachers who wanted us to learn with, from, and for us. The education we hope for is really their vision.

This work also sits between us and the students we have learned with, from, and for over the last several decades. I (Clif) have long loved learning every bit as much as teaching, but over time a growing number of students in my courses have called for blending teaching and learning—learning together. In light of those calls and the MSI study, I have come to embrace a wide range of practices to support collaborative learning—such as co-teaching with students—and to consistently seek to inspire others in higher education to engage in shared problem-solving that contributes to the lives of others. I (Todd) picture in particular two African American students in Cleveland who tried to show me that the way they wrote and thought already helped their college classmates and their teacher write and think better, more completely, more innovatively. They made me finally dissatisfied with improving predominantly white undergraduate education, pushed me to deconstruct my practice, to try to be a collaborative learner.

Finally, this work is owned in part by our partners, Julia and Linda, who have waited for us to step back from our looking at screens and books and talking and listening to students and teachers, trying to piece together a different approach to being a learner and teacher. Both Julia and Linda know better than we do about the power of being with and for others. What goes around, comes around.

Undergraduate Education
for Twenty-First-Century America

This book is rooted in a collaboration that we launched in the summer of 2011 when we began meeting students, faculty, staff, and administrators at twelve Minority-Serving Institutions (MSIs). These colleges and universities provided the foundation of a three-year study of MSIs in the United States (Conrad and Gasman 2015). The Tribal Colleges and Universities (TCUs), Hispanic-Serving Institutions (HSIs), Historically Black Colleges and Universities (HBCUs), and Asian American Native American Pacific Islander Institutions (AANAPIs) in the study had established programs and practices that were advancing the learning, progress, and success of mostly minority students. Over the next three years, our engagement with the MSIs deepened as we— researchers at the University of Wisconsin–Madison and our colleagues at the University of Pennsylvania—interviewed and shadowed students, staff, and faculty on the campuses of these twelve institutions.

Early in the MSIs study we spoke with an administrator at the College of Menominee Nation (CMN) who emphasized that

Predominantly White Institutions (PWIs) in Wisconsin and nationwide were failing to educate Native American STEM (science, technology, engineering, and mathematics) students. The Tribe needed Native scientists and engineers to help "run things around here" and "make decisions" on the Reservation. To address this challenge, he and his colleagues were mapping out a "different approach" to undergraduate education for students majoring in STEM fields by inviting them to and supporting them in networks of students and teachers who learned together as they tackled "local problems" on the Menominee Reservation.

Fueled by our visit to CMN and the other MSIs in the study, the two of us found ourselves comparing notes on park benches in Sacramento and San Diego, a barbeque joint in El Paso, and along a walking trail in Seattle. We talked again and again about the ways in which the MSIs were rewriting the script for undergraduate education. We came to view this script as anchored in collaborative learning—a nontraditional and very different approach to undergraduate education.

Over the next few years we continued to reflect on our visits to the MSIs. As we combed through transcripts and program descriptions and interacted with each other, we were struck by the ways in which the MSIs took a different approach to undergraduate education. The idea of a college education at the MSIs seemed to grow out of a recognition that programs designed in PWIs could not serve minoritized students without first being hacked. These colleges and universities were rewriting the basic code of undergraduate education, institutional cultures, and participant roles as well as the basic structures of programs ranging from remedial math and first-year experience programs to STEM degrees. The MSIs expected their students to be successful in spaces that did not require them to assimilate to mainstream institutional cultures and practices in higher education. These institutions were abandoning top-down pedagogies and assessments that motivated students to place self over relationships and to envision their education as a competition among students in their pursuit of individual achievement. While they were committed to supporting the progress of students who chose to pursue degrees within mainstream higher education, the MSIs described student success in terms of hope, pride in learning, learning both with and for others, and seizing opportunities to contribute to their communities and the lives of others.

Committed to educating students from communities that higher education in this nation has systematically excluded, the MSIs had adopted and were experimenting with programs and practices that run counter to the longstanding tradition of individualistic and competitive education in mainstream higher education. That tradition has failed many students—especially minoritized students—and has fallen short of preparing students for the world of the twenty-first century. The MSIs were redefining traditional roles and responsibilities of students and staff as well as the ways in which they understood and talked about student success in undergraduate education.

To welcome and support minority students in college and contribute to the well-being of the communities from which students come, the MSIs expected students, staff, and faculty to engage in what we refer to as collaborative learning. Collaborative learning, as we define it, is fundamentally different from cooperation and collaboration, where roles and responsibilities are distributed among group participants. In contrast, in collaborative learning, everyone is an active participant in joint problem-solving. Group members engage in back-and-forth dialog in working together to frame shared problems and in coming up with promising ideas to solve them. Everyone is learning both "with and from" others. In concert with joint problem-solving in which networks of participants are learning with and from others, collaborative learners are addressing real-world problems facing communities and beyond: learning *for* others. As elaborated on in the second chapter, we define collaborative learning as when two or more people learn *from*, *with*, and *for* others in shared problem-solving that addresses real-world challenges and opportunities.

As we came to understand and appreciate the widely shared commitment to collaborative learning at the MSIs, we began to contrast the experiences of students at the MSIs with those at other institutions we have studied and at which we have taught. The American undergraduate education that we know echoes time-honored American ideals of freedom and independence. For most students, attaining a bachelor's degree is a solitary journey. Anchored in the freedom to pursue their pathway through college and the widely shared view of college as a private good, most students—under the guidance of faculty, staff, and parents—view individual achievement as the cornerstone of the undergraduate experience.

Without question, the "freedom" for students to pursue their dreams has long played and will continue to play a prominent role in undergraduate education. After all, the right to "life, liberty, and the pursuit of happiness" is at the core of the American narrative. College in America is a way for individuals to get ahead. Writing about American education in 1955, the American economist Milton Friedman could safely "assume" that "a society takes the freedom of the individual, or more realistically the family, as its ultimate objective" and that education is best structured as a "voluntary exchange of individuals" through which each person makes choices that maximize their individual welfare (123–25). But does a college education that is mostly a private journey in which students are driven by the pursuit of individual achievement—and closely aligned with that, personal and material gain—serve students, their communities, our democracy, and the rapidly changing world of the twenty-first century?

The driving purpose of this book is to reimagine the conventional understanding that individual learning should be placed at the forefront of student success in college. We argue that positioning individual learning as the cornerstone of a college education falls far short of educating students not only to thrive in their personal lives but also to thrive and contribute in their workplace and their public lives. Instead, we propose placing collaborative learning at the center of a college education: educate students to become shared problem-solvers who are equipped to take up challenges facing our communities, nation and rapidly changing world, including food shortages, childhood poverty, inequality, political polarization, and our deteriorating environment.

The programs and practices we studied at the twelve MSIs offer promising pathways forward. In our visits to these institutions and our interactions with students, staff, and faculty, we came to appreciate how they have differentiated themselves from most PWIs. The MSIs were redefining the undergraduate experience in large part as a shared endeavor designed to sustain students and their communities. A campus-wide commitment to collaboration was deeply embedded in each of the MSIs we visited: participants were learning together and learning for others through shared problem-solving that addressed real-world challenges and opportunities in their lives, the lives of members of their communities, and far beyond. Students, staff, and faculty at the MSIs spoke freely about the ways in which they and surrounding communities viewed the purpose of undergraduate education, the barriers to student success that are wired into much of American higher education, and what fosters student success as they define it. Many expressed pride in being part of an institution that enrolled students from communities that were traditionally excluded from higher education, and they were proud to be associated with an institution that embraced a shared vision of student success.

Placing collaborative learning at the forefront of student success in college was embedded in the MSIs. These institutions were invested in building and sustaining relationships in which students, faculty, and staff routinely engage one another for purposes of advancing the learning as well as the persistence of all students. Interdependence trumped independence and competition and, in turn, programs and practices were designed to support students in developing give-and-take connections with faculty, staff, and other students, and contributing to a campus-wide culture in which everyone was expected to participate and contribute. By creating interdependent and inclusive networks, these MSIs not only recognized but valued and drew on the diverse voices, identities, and life experiences that students bring to campus. Racial and ethnic perspectives that are often excluded in mainstream higher education clearly mattered at these institutions. And by imagining collaborative learning at the forefront of student success in college, much of it focused on solving problems in local communities, all twelve of the MSIs had not only created institutional cultures but also implemented programs and practices that engage students in collaborative learning.

To be sure, the institutions in the MSI study as well as other institutions that have incorporated collaboration and cooperation into the undergraduate experience have been influenced in part by the findings of decades of research on interactive group work: when students have opportunities to engage in learning with peers, they tend to learn more, learn more deeply, and learn skills for interacting with others (Barkley, Major, and Cross 2014; Springer, Stanne, and Donovan 1999). The MSIs established programs that scaffold collaboration—such as math emporia, first-year experiences, bridge programs, tutoring, and peer review—in part because these programs have been shown to support the learning and the persistence of students. They expect students to learn together and to support students who have been told they are unprepared for college with the opportunity to see themselves as learners with something to contribute.

We have come to see that placing collaborative learning anchored in shared problem-solving at the heart of the undergraduate experience has the potential not only to strengthen but also to disrupt the commitment to individual learning as the keystone to student success in college. Why? Programs and practices at the MSIs as well as in some PWIs that have caught our attention are not stopping at incorporating interactive group learning to increase the engagement, motivation, and learning of individual learners. These institutions are mashing up group-learning strategies, intentionally and unintentionally engaging students with one another as well as with staff and faculty members in what the MSIs have variously named as "hubs," "networks," "organically forming cohorts," and "learning communities." In programs that these institutions have rolled out, the success of individual students depends on everyone learning to contribute to and sustain networks by drawing on their experiences, identities, and voices—and valuing those of others. The success of programs depends on offering an education in which every learner is asked and expected to find modes of participation that empower them to become active participants in collaborative learning. Collaborative learning techniques serve as a means to knit together interdependent networks of learners who are engaged in pursuing promising ideas that address shared problems.

As we looked closely at practices within and beyond the MSIs, we saw an approach to education that values the interests and commitments of individuals while, at the same time, asking all participants to be learners who accept the opportunity and obligation to deliberate on what everyone brings to the table. Rather than emphasizing the interests of individuals or inculcating the values of one or another group, an education anchored in collaborative learning scaffolds a process through which participants draw on and enrich—confirm, elaborate, and revise— the search for promising ideas to address shared problems. Educational spaces that support collaborative learning invite and support everyone to reflect on their contributions to shared endeavors.

Six years after we first met students, staff, and faculty at the MSIs, we launched this book project based on ongoing conversations in which we reflected on the commitment to interdependence and solving shared problems at the MSIs. This book traces our exploration, drawing not only on what we learned from our visits to the institutions in the MSIs study but also on what emerged as we reflected on our own experiences in higher education and sifted through the research and literature on undergraduate education. The MSIs played the role of catalyst and provided much of the data for this book.

Not infrequently, our visits to the MSIs confronted us with the limitations of our positionality. Both of us came to the study through careers that included direct investments in making undergraduate education more inclusive and more equitable. Clif, who has been a professor at four PWIs, has spent more than three decades as an expert witness in major civil rights cases that have addressed the vestiges of segregation in American higher education. Todd has been a composition instructor and staff member at open-enrollment colleges who came to the University of Wisconsin–Madison to study higher education as a social institution that seemed designed to exclude most students in the community colleges at which he had taught. While we both began the study envisioning undergraduate education as mostly a space in which students pursue their individual goals, the people we met at the MSIs gently and not so gently, directly and indirectly, invited us to reckon with how we imagined student success. Leaders and staff at TCUs, for example, told us "frankly" that some of our questions prejudged their programs based on mainstream norms in American higher education, norms set by PWIs. "We are," as one administrator put it, "a different kind of cat."

In our visits to these institutions, students, faculty, staff, and administrators talked about a college education as not only providing a wide range of benefits for students but also cultivating a commitment to serving the minoritized people and groups within their institution and in off-campus communities. What permeated every story was the shared understanding of their college as "our college" and the shared belief that, as an administrator at the College of Menominee Nation put it, "the success of the group is more important than the success of any single individual in the group."

The people we met at the MSIs often emphasized that their campus-wide ethos of interdependence, tethered to joint problem-solving, contributed to students finding a sense of belonging and becoming genuinely engaged in learning. Many of the students we spoke with who had previously attended a PWI were forthcoming about often feeling like misfits at the PWI they had attended. In comparison, their experiences at their MSI were fueled in large measure by an education anchored in networks of students, staff, and faculty who valued the identities and experiences that each participant brought to campus. Students we interviewed described themselves as valued participants in an educational community in which they were expected to contribute to the success of their peers and engage in opportunities to become involved in real-world problem-solving. Undergraduate education at the MSIs, to a large extent, was about making space in which every student felt able and obligated to contribute both on and off-campus through collaborative problem-solving.

The MSIs and other institutions that welcome minority students, either by design or by necessity, are reworking the mainstream blueprint for undergraduate education. These institutions are providing opportunities for students to pursue their dreams in college and beyond by participating in networks of students, staff, and faculty that provide space for diverse participants to work together—capitalizing on their differences—in addressing shared problems. While the MSIs we visited did not broadcast "collaborative learning," students, staff, and faculty often described institutional cultures and roles that empowered participants to learn together and expected that participants embrace the commitment to contribute to the lives of others. Our visits to the MSIs planted the seed that led us to elevate the importance of collaborative learning in undergraduate education and to explore its implications for reenvisioning mainstream culture and practices for educating our diverse nation.

Two decades into the twenty-first century, we see relatively few opportunities at most colleges and universities for students, staff, and faculty to learn together. To be sure, most colleges and universities provide opportunities for collaboration and cooperative learning. But opportunities for students to become collaborative learners—such as engaging in research or community-based learning—are not woven into the undergraduate experience for most students in American colleges and universities.

Leaving aside pockets of collaborative learning as well as cooperative learning, faculty and staff at most colleges and universities design students' learning experiences around the conventional definition of student success. The longstanding emphasis on individual learning and achievement as the measure of student success is reflected in the literature on college student development along with the scholarship on student success (Astin 1993; Chickering and Reisser 1993; Kegan 1982; Kohlberg 1976; Kuh, Schuh, and Whitt 1991; Pascarella and Terenzini 2005; Tinto 2005). This conventional definition of student success finds expression in colleges and universities in myriad ways—from mission statements to institutional policies to the everyday rhetoric and behavior of faculty, staff, students, and administrators. At most institutions, course syllabi, teaching and learning practices, and testing and grading practices are closely aligned with the development and achievement of individuals. Relatively few institutions place primary emphasis on educating students to become shared problem-solvers who embrace the commitment to contribute in local communities and far beyond.

Drawing on our experiences at MSIs, we have come to believe that it is not only possible but necessary to place collaborative learning at the forefront of student success in twenty-first-century undergraduate education. To that end, the animating purpose of this book is to unsettle the placement of individual learning and achievement as the bedrock of a college education. Instead, we propose an alternative script for a college education, including programs, courses, and pedagogy. This script places collaborative learning—learning from, with, and for others—at the forefront of student success in college.

We divide the book into two parts. In part one we question the preeminence of individual learning and achievement as the driver of a college education. In the first of two chapters we challenge the narrative that individual learning is sufficient to prepare students to flourish and contribute in their workplace, public, and personal lives. We suggest that most colleges and universities are placing relatively little emphasis on educating students to embrace interdependence and the collective pursuit of promising ideas for addressing challenges and seizing opportunities throughout their lives and the lives of others. In so doing, they are marginalizing the importance of educating students to learn not only from others but also with others, and to embrace a lifelong commitment to contribute to our pluralistic and interdependent communities, nation, and world.

In the second chapter we make the case for placing collaborative learning at the forefront of student success in college. We begin the chapter by proposing that our colleges and universities should be educating collaborative learners—students who are committed and prepared to learn from, with, and for others in cultivating ideas to apply in their workplace, public, and personal lives. After exploring calls for collaboration, cooperation, and teamwork, we conclude that the contemporary literature falls short of advancing a compelling definition of collaborative learning that is driven by core practices to ignite, nourish, and sustain networks of collaborative learners. Using our definition and core practices as a point of reference, we argue that collaborative learning remains on the margins of the undergraduate experience for most students. We conclude the chapter by advancing our argument for placing collaborative learning as the cornerstone of a college education and recognizing the need for institutional transformation at most institutions of higher learning if collaborative learning is to be placed at the forefront of student success.

In part two we propose four pathways to foster collaborative learning: (1) cultivate an institutional culture that places collaborative learning as the cornerstone of the undergraduate experience; (2) blend roles and responsibilities of faculty, staff, and students; (3) adopt practices for receiving and giving feedback on problem-solving; and (4) anchor the curriculum in shared problem-solving. Each of these pathways identifies and elaborates on programs and practices for empowering students to embrace the freedom and the responsibility to join with others in shared problem-solving. We identified these four pathways based on our experiences as students, teachers, and administrators in higher education; our research; relevant literature; and examples of collaborative learning at our nation's colleges and universities—examples from not only MSIs but also PWIs.

As we winnowed through promising practices at the MSIs along with those in mainstream higher education, we were struck by how transformative collaborative learning is for American undergraduate education. Institutions that promote shared problem-solving often brand collaborative programs and practices as unique and nontraditional. Adopting practices that incorporate collaborative learning throughout the undergraduate experience often disrupts and overhauls traditional teaching and learning practices. As Kenneth Bruffee (1993) put it more than a quarter of a century ago: "Collaborative learning is not just another arrow in a teacher's quiver of pedagogical tricks. It requires teachers to subordinate and transform traditional teaching methods" (9). We invite faculty, staff, and students to disrupt many traditional teaching and learning practices and place collaborative learning at the heart of undergraduate education, thereby opening spaces for all the stakeholders in undergraduate education to learn together.

CHAPTER 1

Unsettling Individual Learning as the Cornerstone of a College Education

Individual learning—learning focused on individual achievement that provides students with the knowledge and skills that will give them personal advantage in the workplace and beyond—has long been the cornerstone of a college education. This began with the establishment of our nation's first college in 1636. In this chapter, we reflect on ways in which mainstream culture and practices at most colleges and universities continue to anchor undergraduate education in individual learning and achievement. We conclude the chapter with our argument that individual learning should no longer be at the forefront of student success in college in the twenty-first century.

The Dominance of Individual Learning

From the founding of Harvard College in 1636 until well into the nineteenth century, the undergraduate experience was anchored in the pursuit of individual learning in the liberal arts and sciences. In 1828, the Yale Report formalized individual learning as the driving purpose of a college education. The Yale faculty declared that the overarching purpose of a college education is "the discipline and furniture of the mind: expanding its powers and storing it with knowledge." Fueled in part by the Morrill Act (Land Grant Act) of 1862, the late nineteenth century saw the rise of the utilitarian-vocational model of a college education with the introduction of a wide range of professional programs in such fields as engineering and agriculture. In *An Aristocracy of Everyone: The Politics of Education and the Future of America*, Benjamin Barber (1992) suggested that there are two prominent and diametrically opposed models of undergraduate education: the purist (liberal education) and the vocational. The purist emphasizes learning for its own sake, while the vocational (professional) emphasizes learning that prepares students for the workplace. Both the purist and the vocational (professional) place primary emphasis on the education of individuals.

The emphasis in American higher education on individual learning—the freedom to pursue one's learning without embracing the opportunity to learn from and with others as well as the responsibility to learn for others—has been consolidating since the Morrill Act. Shortly after the Civil War ended in 1865, an increased emphasis on individual learning and achievement in our colleges and universities was driven by the introduction of the elective system. In his inaugural address at Harvard University in 1869, President Charles Eliot introduced the elective system so that students would be given the "freedom" to choose most of their undergraduate courses. Echoing this initiative, since that time most of our nation's colleges have established elective systems in which students have the "freedom" to pursue their journey as individual learners.

Public discourse pitting the general-liberal against the utilitarian-vocational has been accompanied by the widely cherished success story of American higher education: providing access to higher education for a rapidly growing population to enjoy the individual benefits of a college education. Between the end of the Civil War in 1865 and the end of World War II in 1945, the American population grew by roughly 250 percent; meanwhile, college enrollment grew by 2,500 percent. Near the end of World War II, policymakers consolidated this transformation through the Servicemen's Readjustment Act (1944), which essentially proclaimed higher education as the primary job preparation system in our nation. Over the next several decades, federal legislation—including the Civil Rights Act (1964), the Higher Education Act (1965), the establishment of Title V and Title IX (1972), and the Americans with Disabilities Act (1990)—opened access to our colleges and universities for many Americans. Between 1940 and 1990 enrollment in higher education grew by roughly 800 percent.

As more students came to college, undergraduate education has been increasingly branded as a private good that prepares students for "jobs, jobs, jobs," and the cost of college has risen dramatically. Colleges and universities have become an integral part of the workforce development structure in the United States (Carnevale, Smith, and Strohl 2010), and most students see their college education as a pipeline to a position in the job market. This market-driven ethos has reinforced the centrality of individual achievement throughout the college experience. Most students view college as a private good in which their learning is targeted at acquiring a personal store of knowledge and skills that will lead to a credential and "competitive advantage"

(Zemsky 2005). College, for the majority of students, has become a solo and efficient expedition in which "individual learning" leads to degrees that have value in a labor market. The US Department of Education College Scorecard emphasizes costs, completion rates, financial aid and debt, and salary after completing a field of study.

While the dominant emphasis on individual achievement and learning in our nation's colleges and universities is rarely contested, it is important to note that many institutions—from private liberal arts colleges to flagship public universities—have incorporated pockets of collaborative learning. To illustrate, Alexander Meiklejohn introduced the Experimental College at the University of Wisconsin–Madison in 1927. The Experimental College, "a college within a college" in which faculty and students shared living quarters in lakeshore dorms, established its own rules. These rules included six-week modules instead of semesters and no conventional grades. A self-governing community that was established in part as a community which embraced higher education as a public good no less than a private good, the Experimental College had a "unified" two-year curriculum and close ties between faculty and students, who were viewed as "co-equal partners" (Nelson 2001, 135). The Experimental College was dissolved in 1932, but it became the precursor of the Integrated Liberal Studies program that continues to be a vibrant program at the University of Wisconsin–Madison. Both the Experimental College and the Integrated Liberal Studies program incorporated collaboration and a commitment to a community of learners. Notwithstanding such pockets of innovation, individual achievement continues to be the cornerstone of a college education across most of our nation's colleges and universities.

Mainstream Culture and Practices: College as Opportunity for Individual Learning

The longstanding emphasis on individual learning, which reflects American ideals of individual liberty and self-determination, remains at the heart of the undergraduate experience. Mainstream culture and practices at most colleges and universities invite students to embrace their personal development and achievement as the unifying narrative of the college experience. At the undergraduate level, institutions adopt curriculum requirements, teaching and learning practices, and extracurricular opportunities that support each student on their journey, though college and faculty are encouraged to customize students' learning experiences. Traditional pedagogies—lecturing in particular—are often accompanied by blended learning, active learning, simulations, and personalized learning. These pedagogies are typically designed to promote individual students' learning and achievement. Significantly, most student assessment in higher education—from placement testing to classroom evaluations and grading—remains focused on measuring the achievement of individuals.

Not surprisingly, the outcomes that matter most in contemporary American higher education are degrees awarded, the performance of graduates on licensure examinations, loan default rates, graduate employment rates, and other indicators that demonstrate return on investment for individuals (Cohen and Kisker 2010, 549–54). Most stakeholders in American higher education, both within and outside colleges and universities, define access to undergraduate education for students as the opportunity to acquire the knowledge and skills that will benefit them throughout their lives. By the beginning of the twenty-first century, whether they chose a general-liberal or utilitarian-vocational pathway, the majority of students had come to see college as mostly about getting a good job (Autor 2014; Baum, Ma, and Payea 2013; Gallup Inc. 2014; Morin, Brown, and Fry 2014). As the sociologist David Labaree (1997) put it, most students think that the primary purpose of college is for them to "get ahead." While hardly new (Grubb and Lazerson 2005) and still contested (National Task Force on Civic Learning and Democratic Engagement 2012; Rosenbaum 2001), the success story of American higher education is a story of providing access for students to be successful in their pursuit of social mobility. That story ends with students obtaining credentials that come with the economic, social, and cultural capital that makes them competitive in whatever pathways they choose to pursue—such as securing employment upon graduation or pursuing a graduate degree.

Most college students today are "bowling alone" (Putnam 2000). They come to college to develop transferable knowledge and skills, and college is structured as opportunities to develop their personal store of capital. Not infrequently, students market themselves to faculty and administrators during their undergraduate journey—not only when they are exploring the job market. They compete for opportunities to do research, shadow professionals, and join initiatives on and off campus. Upon graduation, and often with a fistful of supporting documents, they seek to "follow their dreams." Joel Levin and Aida Aliyeva (2015) brought attention to the heightened focus on "self" in higher education as captured in their concept of "embodied neoliberalism," which is engrained in the focus on individual learning and achievement.

What is the conventional justification for individual learning as the dominant narrative of a college education? A college education focused on individual learning empowers students by providing them with opportunities and degrees that are prerequisites for the jobs and futures to which they aspire. As reflected in mainstream culture and practices in American higher education, college is viewed across our nation primarily as an engine of upward mobility.

The Shortcomings of Placing Individual Learning at the Forefront of Student Success

While the acquisition of knowledge and skills through individual learning will continue to play a prominent place in undergraduate education, it is long past time to question the understanding that individual learning is sufficient to prepare students to thrive and to contribute not only in the workplace but throughout their personal and public lives. For several reasons we suggest that the dominant emphasis on individual learning should no longer be at the forefront of student success in college.

First, reflecting the ideal of individualism embedded in Western culture, in most colleges and universities students view their education as competition with one another for grades and opportunities, and mutually reinforcing learning and teaching remains on the margins of the college experience. Put simply, the mainstream emphasis on individual learning fails to appreciate the magnitude of learning both *from* and *with* others. Far too often, students are deprived of opportunities to learn *from* one another by drawing on their diverse perspectives—including differences in their perspectives based on their racial, ethnic, and cultural backgrounds as well as their life experiences. In mainstream higher education, undergraduate students too rarely have opportunities to benefit from feedback from others—such as feedback on an idea they are exploring in a research project. Opportunities for peer review notwithstanding, with few exceptions students are expected to learn from teachers.

Closely aligned with the relatively little emphasis placed on learning from others, the dominant focus on individual learning undermines the value and the importance of students learning *with* others: learning to build interdependent relationships and networks in which participants validate one another as "teachers" and as "learners" and, in turn, strengthen their capabilities for engaging in joint problem-solving. Students are asked to do group work but find little space to learn how to collaborate and, in turn, too rarely experience the benefits of collaborating with others in joint problem-solving. Despite findings from research in social neuroscience about the superiority of collective problem-solving for developing promising ideas (Wolf Shenk 2014), undergraduates continue to learn mostly alone.

Nowhere are the limitations of individual problem-solving more evident than in the workplace. As our economy has shifted from industrial production and manufacturing to an economy driven by innovations such as artificial intelligence, American workers are being replaced by computers, robots, and cheaper labor. Employers are relying less on hiring individuals who work autonomously than on hiring people who are prepared to engage in shared problem-solving. In *Teaming: How Organizations Learn, Innovate, and Compete in the Global Economy*, Amy Edmondson (2012) draws on two decades of research on organizations as "complex adaptive systems" to advocate a shift from "command-and-control management" and "bounded group structure" to "teaming," which "brings people together to generate new ideas, find answers, and solve problems" (24). To prepare students for the twenty-first century workplace, our colleges and universities need to place far more emphasis on educating students for careers in which they are prepared to engage in joint problem-solving that leads to innovative solutions to real-world problems (Friedman 2011). No less significant, the potential benefits of joint problem-solving extend across our lives—from the workplace to our public and our personal lives.

Second, the emphasis on individual learning leads students to embrace self-interested individualism in which their "individual and social agency is defined largely through market-driven notions of individualism, competition, and consumption" (Grioux 2002, 426). Relatively little emphasis is placed on encouraging students not only to learn from one another and learn together but also to learn *for* others. This ethos of freedom without responsibility to others absolves students from engaging in socially relevant problem-solving and embracing a "civic consciousness" through participating in real-world problem-solving that can generate promising ideas that contribute to our world.

We live in communities, a nation, and a world in which challenges and opportunities are constantly emerging. Together, we face growing social inequalities, political divisions, and environmental challenges. Notwithstanding service-learning opportunities in many colleges and universities, the dominant emphasis on individual learning places relatively little emphasis on students embracing a lifelong obligation to take on shared challenges and contribute to the lives of others from the local and regional to the national and global levels. For more than three decades, colleges and universities have struggled with ways to incorporate civic learning and democratic engagement into undergraduate education (National Task Force on Civic Learning and Democratic Engagement 2012).

In falling short with respect to educating students to embrace the commitment and develop the capabilities to collaborate with others in developing solutions to shared problems, the widespread emphasis on individual learning is not adequately preparing students to be contributors in our democracy. While many colleges and universities are variously engaged with communities, civic learning and democratic engagement remain optional at most institutions. In turn, undergraduate education does not support most students in becoming citizens who genuinely listen to one another and draw on diverse voices in the pursuit of promising ideas for addressing shared problems. Most graduates have not developed the civic literacies they need to navigate and push back against the political tribalism (Chua 2018), polarization (Klein 2020), and the abundant presence of "true believers"—"the person of fanatical faith who is ready to sacrifice his life for a holy cause" (Hoffer 1951, xii).

Third, the emphasis on "me" over "we" and the expectation that students adopt the identity of an individual learner can be inhospitable, even hostile, for many students. This is especially the case for students who have been raised in families and communities that accentuate responsibility to others as much as responsibility to oneself. In his research on factors that support the success of students of color, Samuel Museus (2011) draws on a growing body of literature that explores the ways in which collectivist organizational cultures may support the success of students of color and competitive individualist cultures may promote their departure. In her research on American Indians, Sasanehsaeh Pyawasay (2017, 18) found that their success in college is less about social mobility and personal gain and more about helping their communities. Caught between two worlds during college—and unable to reconcile the colonial-industrial definition of success as individual achievement with their longing for community—Native American students and many other traditionally underrepresented students are provided too few opportunities at mainstream colleges and universities to draw on their cultural backgrounds and identities. It is not surprising that faced with the choice of whether to assimilate into mainstream culture and abandon the core values of their home culture, many traditionally underrepresented students choose to leave college before graduation and return to their home communities.

In our visits to MSIs, we listened to student after student reflect on the ways in which some of their professors at Predominantly White Institutions (PWIs) were blind to the value of creating and sustaining community both within and outside of class. They described courses and programs that left them feeling singled out and isolated. Many students recounted having to create their own communities to advance their learning and talk through the relevance of what they were learning to their lives and their home communities. Some students told us that they had transferred to an MSI in part because many of the people at the PWI they had attended seemed indifferent to their cultural identities and their desire for supportive networks. Not infrequently, they transferred because the literacies and cultural ways of learning that they brought to a PWI were expected to be left behind. Many people we spoke with at MSIs portrayed their educational experiences at PWIs as failing to meet the needs of a "browning America" (King 1991).

In the United States in 2017, twenty-six million students of color represented 53 percent of the 50 million students enrolled in grades K–12 (US Department of Education 2017). Significantly, researchers have found that a dominant focus on independence in college tends to undermine the academic performance of first-generation college students (Stephens et al. 2012)—the majority of whom are students of color. If our colleges and universities are to serve our increasingly diverse nation, collaborative learning should be embedded throughout the college experience.

In the turbulent environment of the twenty-first century, there have been highly visible and repeated calls and protests for equity and social justice across our nation. In a divided society in which opportunity is distributed unevenly, our colleges and universities need to provide spaces in which all students can learn and learn together. We envision undergraduate education as a kind of sandbox in which students learn "problem-solving, critical and creative thinking, working in groups" and practice being democratic citizens (Commission on the Future of Undergraduate Education 2017). Yet most institutions continue to embrace an individualistic system that, at most, sets up collaboration as voluntary cooperation of individuals; this poorly serves most minority students. Most colleges and universities are, for the most part, failing to adequately serve traditionally underrepresented students—as reflected in the persistent gaps in college outcomes (such as persistence rates and graduation rates) between white and minority students.

In summary, guided by the myth that individual learning is enough and committed to providing students with opportunities to accrue status and capital for their personal advancement and individual welfare, most of our nation's colleges and universities are, far too often, falling short of educating all students to learn *from*, *with*, and *for* others. Undergraduate education, by failing to provide students frequent and regular opportunities to cultivate their capabilities to engage in shared problem-solving, is not adequately preparing most students to participate fully and flourish in their personal, public, and workplace lives. In embracing individual learning over collaborative learning, most colleges and universities are falling short of educating our diverse nation. If we are to provide equitable opportunities for all college students, including Black, Latina/o, Native American, Asian American and Pacific Islander students, and all other underrepresented populations, the time has come to disrupt the dominant emphasis on individual learning and place collaborative learning as the driver of the undergraduate experience.

CHAPTER 2

A Twenty-First-Century Imperative

Placing Collaborative Learning at the Forefront
of Student Success

Nearly a century ago, John Dewey (1938) proposed that schools should connect the learning experiences of students to their everyday lives through problem-solving that prepares them not only for employment but also for their lives as citizens. In the run up to the twenty-first century there was a growing chorus of voices recommending that problem-solving should be at the core of a college education. In 1998 the Boyer Commission on Educating Undergraduates in the Research University argued that "inquiry, investigation, and discovery are at the heart" of the educational journey for undergraduates. Smith et al. (2004, 9) pointed to seven major reports on undergraduate education reform published between 1998 and 2002, each of which recommended that undergraduate education be designed to ensure that novice college students have a range of opportunities to construct new knowledge. More recently, Conrad and Dunek (2020) proposed that undergraduate education should place primary emphasis on educating "inquiry-driven learners": people who are equipped with the capabilities to explore and cultivate promising ideas in their workplace, public, and personal lives.

In this chapter we advance our rationale for placing collaborative learning at the core of a college education in which students join and contribute to inclusive networks that are addressing shared problems. The chapter begins with our highlighting contemporary calls for collaboration, cooperation, and teamwork. We then advance a definition of collaborative learning along with a set of core practices for empowering students, staff, and faculty to propel, nourish, and sustain shared problemsolving. After suggesting that collaborative learning remains on the margins of the undergraduate experience, we conclude with our justification for incorporating collaborative learning throughout undergraduate education and our call for institutional transformation.

Calls for Collaboration, Cooperation, and Teamwork

Along with placing the education of problem-solvers at the forefront of a college education, there have been calls for incorporating cooperation and collaboration into the undergraduate curriculum for decades. "Develop reciprocity and cooperation among students" was the second of Arthur Chickering and Zelda Gamson's "Seven Principles of Good Practice in Undergraduate Education" (Chickering and Gamson 1987). The Boyer Commission concluded that "collaborative efforts" (22) should be tethered to an undergraduate education anchored in inquiry-based learning. "Active and collaborative learning" was identified as one of five benchmarks of effective educational practice in the National Study of Student Engagement (NSSE) in 2000, and "collaborative learning" remains a NSSE Engagement Indicator and high-impact practice (National Survey of Student Engagement 2014).

Collaboration and teamwork are near the top of most lists of twenty-first century skills that students need to acquire. In 2005, the Association of American Colleges and Universities (AAC&U) advanced the LEAP (Liberal Education and America's Promise) vision of undergraduate education, which has been adopted by many colleges and universities. Under the rubric "intellectual and practical skills," AAC&U identified "teamwork and problem-solving" as a major learning outcome at the undergraduate level (3). Bernie Trilling and Charles Fadel in *21st Century Skills: Learning for Life in Our Times* (Trilling and Fadel 2009, 55) put forward "collaboration" as a key "learning and innovation" skill. In *Education for Life and Work: Developing Transferable Knowledge and Skills in the 21st Century*, the National Research Council (2012) made a similar claim in their meta-analysis of what key skills matter, how they relate to one another and traditional academic content areas, and how they are best learned and taught. "Teamwork and collaboration" were identified as one of two clusters of skills that make up interpersonal competence. The Commission on the Future of Undergraduate Education (2017) places teamwork and collaboration at the center of an undergraduate education.

Along with calls for collaboration and teamwork in undergraduate education, there is a growing body of literature on "collaborative learning" (Barkley, Major, and Cross 2014). In the 1980s and 1990s, Kenneth Bruffee (1999) played a leading role in promoting collaborative learning. In *Collaborative Learning: Higher Education, Interdependence, and the Authority of Knowledge*,

Bruffee challenged the view of education that positions students as lacking competency and cultural capital—"blank slates" who come to college to learn valuable knowledge and skills. Instead of viewing knowledge as "an entity that we transfer from one head to another" and student success as knowledge acquisition, he invited college teachers to embrace collaborative learning and "assume instead that knowledge is a consensus among the members of a community of knowledgeable peers—something people construct by talking together and reaching agreement" (3). Like others (Harris 1989; Trimbur 1989), we wrestle with Bruffee's idealization of consensus and community in ways that fail to account adequately for the role of differences and conflicts among learners. Still, in calling for students to imagine learning as the co-construction of knowledge, Bruffee's book pointed to the need for a succinct and persuasive definition of collaborative learning.

A Definition of Collaborative Learning Aligned with Core Practices

We define collaborative learning as taking place when two or more people learn *from, with*, and *for* others in shared problem-solving that is focused on the pursuit of promising ideas for addressing *real-world challenges and opportunities*. Drawing on the concept of "communities of practice" originally developed by Jean Lave and Etienne Wenger in *Situated Learning* (Lave and Wenger 1991) and expanded upon by Wenger in *Communities of Practice* (Wenger 1999), we envision collaborative learning as taking place in communities where participants are guided by a set of core practices as they work interdependently to develop solutions to shared problems. We propose the following practices to empower group members to ignite, nourish, and sustain collaborative learning:

- Develop a shared endeavor that is anchored in "burning questions" (Harter 2006, 331) that are shared by everyone in the group, that all participants are passionate about pursuing, and that crystallize the problem(s) guiding their problem-solving.
- Cultivate a culture of trust, vigilant listening, genuine humility, and respectfulness that honors and draws on the knowledge, analytical capabilities, imaginations, and life experiences of all participants.
- Obligate each member of the group to seize responsibility to engage in spirited back-and-forth dialogue in which they are providing ongoing feedback to one another in developing promising ideas in their shared problem-solving.
- Preserve spaces for diverse and contrarian voices and perspectives from both inside and outside of the group.
- Encourage group members to take the time to self-reflect and share their reflections with the group.
- Question self and others—including group members, authorities, and extant knowledge—throughout their inquiry and, in so doing, embrace uncertainty and risk-taking.
- Hold participants accountable to one another to ensure a shared commitment to problem-solving that contributes to the lives of those outside of their community of practice at the local, regional, national, and/or global level.

These core practices connect participants and sustain relationships in geographical and virtual networks that are at once interdependent and dynamic. To illustrate, in developing a shared agenda for inquiry, participants begin by "asking" one another potential questions to guide their inquiry and then listening rather than by "telling" one another what question(s) they should pursue. In focusing on "asking versus telling" (Schein 2013, 4) and encouraging all participants to speak freely and engage in ongoing questioning and back-and-forth dialogue, collaborative learning fosters a culture anchored in trusting and respectful relationships that, at the same time, values differences and conflicts and invites creativity in identifying and solving the problem(s) at the center of the shared endeavor.

It is worth noting that collaborative learning has similarities with cooperative learning. Both collaborative learning and cooperative learning embrace small group interaction and interdependence, and both place competition between group participants on the margins. For more than three decades researchers have found that group learning in which students work with one another in problem-solving enhances student learning more than teaching strategies that do not make use of groups. Hundreds of studies have found that cooperative learning and collaboration have positive benefits for individuals: motivating students, encouraging positive relationships with students and faculty, and enhancing individual achievement (Astin 1987, 17; Barkley, Major, and Cross 2014, 25–27; Johnson, Johnson, and Smith 2014; Springer, Stanne, and Donovan 1999).

While there is overlap between cooperative learning and collaborative learning, we suggest that they also differ from one another. Cooperative learning is the well-established instructional use of small groups to promote positive interdependence among students in completing assignments (Johnson, Johnson, and Smith 2014). In cooperative learning, each individual in a group accepts their roles and their responsibilities. In contrast to cooperative learning, collaborative learning is anchored in participation in a network in which all members—sometimes including instructors and staff members—hold one another accountable as they join together in framing shared problems and working together in solving them. Collaborative learning often involves taking on local problems, and roles and responsibilities evolve as group members listen to, challenge, and provide feedback to one another. In so doing, collaborative learning positions participants to establish and sustain relationships and adopt and relinquish roles as they learn not only from one another but also with one another and for others. Collaborative learning emphasizes heterogeneity by drawing on diverse voices and perspectives to enrich and sustain the search for promising ideas (McPherson, Smith-Lovin, and Cook 2013).

Collaborative Learning on the Margins

Most colleges and universities create opportunities for students to interact with one another in groups. And a growing number of undergraduate students pursue opportunities to engage in team-based learning, community-based learning, service-learning, and research. While we do not know how often these opportunities are designed for students to learn together in shared problem-solving, collaborative learning as we have defined it has clearly gained some footing in higher education over the last several decades. We draw on some of these initiatives in our exploration of pathways to cultivate collaborative learning in the next four chapters. Yet, notwithstanding pockets of collaborative learning in two-year colleges, four-year colleges, liberal arts colleges, and universities, our review of the literature and our experiences in higher education suggest that many of these initiatives are not designed to promote collaborative learning. Most are supplements to mainstream curriculum and instruction that promote individual learning.

Why does collaborative learning remain on the margins of the undergraduate experience for most students? First, because mainstream higher education promotes mainstream American culture and its emphasis on individualism and competition rather than community, programs and pedagogical practices that emphasize collaboration may threaten the existing order, including those in power in top-down hierarchies. For example, incorporating collaborative learning in the classroom may problematize traditional assessment practices such as standardized testing and grading—metrics of individual accomplishment. The practice of "grading on the curve" ranks students such that they are neither encouraged nor rewarded for contributing to the learning of others.

Second, many initiatives in higher education that invite students to work together are designed to scaffold cooperative learning or teamwork that contributes to individual learning. Students are paired with one another or placed in small groups and assigned to work on a project. They divide up tasks—often not meeting in person—and produce pieces of a group project. One person handles the review of literature, another conducts interviews, and still another completes the data analysis. The final paper is a result of individual efforts. While students often engage in cooperation in completing group assignments, often missing are opportunities and the obligation for group members to engage in spirited dialogue with one another through which group participants join together to pursue a shared line(s) of inquiry, constantly challenge one another, and exchange formative feedback with one another in their joint problem-solving.

Third, many group projects place "group bonding" at the center of the experience. As Alan Jacobs (Jacobs 2017) has suggested, a lot of "thinking" in groups is social bonding, not thinking. Drawing on an essay by Marilynne Robinson, Jacobs observed: "Why would people ever think, when thinking deprives them of 'the pleasure of sharing an attitude one knows is socially approved'— especially in an online environment where social approval of one's attitude is so much easier to acquire, in the currency of likes, favors, followers, and friends? And to acquire *instantaneously*" (21). From our perspective and those of others (Barkley, Major, and Cross 2014; Prince 2004), collaboration occurs only within social networks in which participants are learning with and from one another in working toward a shared goal. The verb "collaborate" comes from Latin: "to work together."

Fourth, most calls for "collaboration" redound primarily to the benefit of the individual. For example, the AAC&U Value Rubric for Teamwork states that what matters is "the teamwork of an individual student." Not surprisingly, this emphasis on the individual values what a student contributes over what the interaction produces, valuing individual student achievement over collaborative learning. When two students are paired in a group assignment for purposes of "cooperation and teamwork" to work on a project, each student is often asked to identify the sections that they have written and to evaluate the "cooperation" and "teamwork" of their partner on a rubric that assesses their individual performance on the group project. Students are often driven to contribute to a group project because their grade is on the line.

Notwithstanding calls for collaboration, most of our colleges and universities continue to place primary emphasis on individual learning, and student success is judged mostly on the basis of students' attaining credits, degrees, and jobs. Most students are assimilated into cultures focused on self-attainment that places relatively little emphasis on their learning *with* and *from* others—and *for* others—in the pursuit of promising ideas.

Why Place Collaborative Learning at the Forefront of Student Success?

College students live, and will continue to live, in a constantly changing world—from the personal to the local to the global. As graduates they will face a range of formidable challenges as well as opportunities across the landscapes of their lives. These challenges will rarely be tame problems that are "definable, understandable, and consensual" (Rittel and Webber 1973, 156). College graduates will take on problems that cannot be addressed in one "correct" way; rather, these challenges will require them to manage missing data, value conflicts, ambiguity, and a host of other uncertainties. As Paul Hanstedt (2018) puts it: "We live in a wicked world, an unpredictable world. We need wicked graduates with wicked competencies" (4). More often than not, personal stores of knowledge and skills and individual "Eureka" moments will be insufficient to empower them to address major challenges and seize opportunities throughout their lives. Collaborative learning must become the cornerstone of the college experience for all students if they are to be educated not only to survive and thrive but to engage with others in shared problem-solving in their workplace, public, and private lives.

As far back as Socrates and the symposiums that he oversaw, the Greeks appreciated the synergistic power of multiple minds working together in addressing a common goal (Bertman 2010). From the Greeks onward, artists and scientists—from

Michelangelo to Newton and Einstein—have found collaborative problem-solving to be more effective than individual problem-solving in the search for promising ideas. As Joshua Wolf Shenk (Wolf Shenk 2014, 1) put it: "[T]he lone genius is a myth that has outlived its usefulness . . . a more truthful model is emerging: the creative network" (6). Productive and creative learners—far more often than not—are collaborative learners (Bruner 1996; Goode et al. 2018; Lave and Wenger 1991; National Research Council 2012; Vygotsky 1962).

If undergraduate education is to prepare students to flourish, all participants—faculty, students, staff, and administrators—must reaffirm that humans learn not only by drawing on their knowledge and experiences but also by exploring ideas with others. To that end, we must guide students to engage those whose "lived experiences" and voices have long been and often continue to be marginalized. The longstanding and dominant emphasis on individual learning often silences the voices of many students. Ironically, while interdependence and collaborative problem-solving are embedded in the families and communities of many traditionally underrepresented students, their potential contributions to shared problem-solving are often lost when individual learning remains at the epicenter of the undergraduate experience.

A college education for the twenty-first century must include a wide range of opportunities for all students to appreciate the value of drawing on the diverse perspectives of others—especially those that differ from their own perspectives. Far too often the public discourse across our nation is dominated by "true believers (Hoffer 1951). What is often missing in the public discourse are the diverse voices of citizens who are engaged in open and respectful dialogue in problem-solving that takes into account the interests and ideas of others. As Amy Chua argues in *Political Tribes: Group Instinct and the Fate of Nations* (2018), the rise of "political tribalism" in the United States is posing a threat to democracy as we have known it, including "who we are" as a nation (166). If we are to realize the ideals of our democracy and the Preamble to the United States Constitution, which emphasizes "we the people" forming a "more perfect" community, we must educate students to be active participants in solving shared problems by weaving collaborative learning throughout the undergraduate experience.

Our nation-state faces formidable challenges—poverty, hate speech, public safety and health, providing accessible and inclusive education, racial inequity, growing social divisions, and bombastic rhetoric in our nation's capital and far beyond. We seem to be approaching many of these challenges by placing our community or our nation ("Us") against other communities or other countries ("Them"). To address such challenges, we need citizens who have learned to embrace and engage diverse viewpoints, including the viewpoints of those citizens with a wide range of cultural, ethnic, political, racial, and socioeconomic backgrounds. Learning to draw on a wide range of perspectives through animated and respectful dialogue that is embedded in collaborative learning can go a long way in preparing students to become robust contributors to collective problem-solving not only in our democracy but throughout their public, workplace, and personal lives as well.

Closely tethered to the ascendency of individual learning as the cornerstone of the college experience, the longstanding rhetoric celebrating college as a "public good" has been superseded by the widely shared belief that college is essentially a "private good" and that citizenship is a "limited good" (Robinson 2016, 31).

Engaging students in collaborative learning in which they are invested in networks of real-world problem-solvers can go a long way in motivating students to transcend themselves and embrace the obligation to contribute to the lives of others—including co-workers, friends and family, and fellow citizens. For example, students in the Full Circle Project at Sacramento State University engage in community service in the 65th Street Corridor Project. Students in this project, anchored in a partnership with primary and secondary schools in a low-income and diverse community, collaborate with one another, faculty, and the community in addressing a wide range of "real-world challenges" facing the community. As they learn in the project, students embrace the commitment to "give back" to the lives of others and describe their education in terms of the health of their communities (Conrad and Gasman 2015, 214–22).

Collaborative learning awakens students to the importance and value of learning *with*, *from*, and *for* others through creating solutions to shared problems. As George Bernard Shaw put it in *Pygmalion*: "Independence? That is middle-class blasphemy. We are all dependent on one another, every soul of us on earth." Our colleges and universities need to provide far more opportunities for students to engage in learning experiences that empower them to join with others in creative and disciplined inquiry and embrace the obligation to "give back" to our communities, nation, and interdependent world.

The Underlying Challenge: Institutional Transformation

Placing collaborative learning—learning that takes place in networks and communities where participants engage in shared problem-solving—at the center of the undergraduate experience calls for institutional transformation. Why? There is widespread agreement that most colleges and universities have not been structured to promote collaboration (Gibbons et al. 1994; Kanter 1994; Kezar 2005; Senge 1990). Most institutions continue to be designed around countless silos that reward individuals; for the most part, rewards are given based on individual accomplishments. Student success is often measured by the rates at which individuals meet entry requirements, persist in their chosen programs, and complete degrees.

Some colleges and universities adopt and sustain a commitment to collaboration. Because collaborative learning runs counter to the dominant focus on individual learning and achievement, the elevation of collaborative learning is transformational for most institutions. Drawing on a study of campuses that reorganized to support collaboration, Adrianna Kezar and Jaime Lester (2009) outlined an organizational process of becoming collaborative. As institutions learn about the benefits of collaboration and recognize the pressure to support and engage in collaboration coming from funders, accreditors, industry partners, and others, they develop structures that create opportunities for students, staff, and faculty to engage in collaboration. In the process, collaborative institutions rewrite core values, missions, and roles and responsibilities.

If collaborative learning is to power our learning and teaching in undergraduate education, it is imperative that interdependence guide the everyday roles and responsibilities of students, faculty, and staff. While many of our nation's colleges and universities provide students with selective opportunities to engage in collaborative learning, such as service-learning experiences and internships, these opportunities are mostly supplementing an undergraduate experience that is focused on individual learning. Routinely embedding undergraduates in networks that are engaged in collaborative problem-solving requires a fundamental redesign of the undergraduate experience—including general education as well as in majors and elective courses.

We have come to see this design work as part of the process of bringing Universal Design (UD) to undergraduate education (Tobin and Behling 2018; Center for Universal Design 1997; CAST 2018). Since architects began designing with accessibility in mind in the 1950s, UD has challenged traditional design frameworks that focus on optimizing products and spaces for average users, arguing instead for designing products and spaces that are welcoming to all potential users. Adopting UD in education has meant designing programs and practices that are "welcoming and useful to groups that are diverse with respect to many dimensions, including gender, race, ethnicity, age, socioeconomic status, ability, veteran status, disability, and learning style" (Burgstahler 2015, 3). Guided by the principles and guidelines developed by the Center for Universal Design (1997) and the Center for Applied Special Technology (CAST) (2018), schools and then colleges and universities have taken on the challenge of designing programs that explicitly value the strengths that participants bring to programs rather than expecting individuals to fit into a conventional educational experience. The aim is an education in which every participant can contribute fully without first acquiring a set of "average" abilities.

As part of bringing the UD framework to education, redesigning undergraduate education around collaborative learning triggers a transformation of the mainstream ways in which students, staff, and faculty work together. Rather than competition in which individuals use predefined abilities to develop portfolios of accomplishments and gain recognition, the education of collaborative learners is designed as opportunities to work with and for others on shared problems. Programs that scaffold collaborative learning guide students to tether their individual status and agency to ensuring that their peers and teachers are as successful as they themselves are. Such revisioning of roles and responsibilities—including those of students with the most dominant cultural and social capital—encourages everyone to make space for and learn from the perspectives of others, including those of students from families with no college experience and students from minoritized groups. Diversity of experiences, identities, interests, and abilities is a necessary condition. This revisioning of roles and responsibilities weaves cross-cultural collaboration and the value of equity and diversity into the fabric of the undergraduate experience.

In redefining educational roles and responsibilities, collaborative learning calls for reframing what undergraduates need to do to succeed in college. This reframing explicitly disrupts mainstream tradition in higher education in which success is closely tethered to assimilation to existing academic and social communities. Rather than scaffolding assimilation or settling for accommodation within an exclusive tradition, collaborative learning asks all participants to view success as contributing to learning through joint problem-solving. Diverse perspectives and abilities are valued, and students are free to find ways to contribute to shared problem-solving instead of focusing on meeting a standardized measure of achievement. Diversity, equity, and inclusiveness are expected, and students' interests and resources shape learning and teaching. While being engaged in collaborative learning, students, staff and faculty adopt fluid and interdependent roles: participants do what is needed for all participants (including themselves) to learn and for real-world problems to get solved. This kind of undergraduate education rewrites college as an invitation to partnerships in which students and teachers talk through how feedback on learning will flow and how it can be customized to value the intentions and the contributions of both newbies and experts as they work together in addressing shared problems.

A commitment to collaborative learning leads to redesigning traditional curriculum and instruction. Classes are structured to be accessible. Teachers and students together establish "conditions for students to learn and display learning"; syllabi communicate "rigor" as difficulty rather than selectivity or inflexibility (Womak 2017, 497). In class, students are positioned as inquirers, people who are prepared to contribute to novel solutions that address shared problems. Students engage in activities, assignments, and assessments that empower them to represent their own interests, beliefs, and knowledge in light of what they are learning in light of the interests, beliefs, and knowledge of others. The goal of instruction is participation in and contribution to complex networks. Rather fitting neatly into class times and rooms, office hours, advising sessions, and the like, collaborative learning calls for constant and multimodal communication. Educational spaces and methods are customized so that learners and teachers have multiple options for participation and routine opportunities for critical reflection on what opportunities to learn are available, how they have engaged these opportunities, and how they might change their participation so as to contribute more fully. Everyone is free to ask their own questions and consider those of others, review multiple approaches to the same problem, and reflect critically on their uses of feedback.

An undergraduate education anchored in collaborative learning does far more than pass on received knowledge. In addition to the known, the curriculum is rich with information about different aspects of performance, processes, partial solutions, and epic wins. It is explicit and co-constructed, and it provides students with opportunities to explain their choice of courses and problems and their role in inquiry as well as to fashion their learning around problems they share with others. Programs that scaffold collaborative learning continually incorporate differences into learning experiences by inquiring into who participants are and what program components might foreclose on the access and participation of the students, staff, and faculty who are participating.

The institutional transformation that we are imagining may come with substantial risks for administrators, faculty, staff, and students. Because student success in most of our colleges and universities is linked to individuals passing classes, completing degrees, and succeeding in what comes next, placing as much emphasis on "we" as on "me" requires institutions and individuals to reimagine everyday life in undergraduate education. Institutions will need to write into recruiting materials, student handbooks, and the curriculum the expectation that students seize responsibility to learn with, from, and for others in solving real-world problems. Staff will need to partner with students and faculty in solving problems in and out of the classroom. Many faculty will need to downsize their control with respect to the ways in which they interact with staff, students, and communities. And, perhaps most important, faculty will need to "share power" with students by embracing interdependence with their students—such as co-teaching with students—and establishing networks among students in which students have the freedom and the responsibility to pursue shared problem-solving.

Chief among the risks for most American colleges and universities is going public with an institutional commitment to antiracist policies, programs, and practices. The institutional transformation called for by collaborative learning requires more than recognizing the value of diversity and providing support for underserved students. Collaborative learning—a give-and-take in which all participants are recognized and are also responsible for recognizing others—rests on valuing differences in backgrounds and experiences and on listening to and drawing on diverse and conflicting voices in framing and solving problems. Practices that limit or work against the full participation of some individuals limit and work against collaborative learning. Practices that value some individuals' needs and contributions over those of others based on their social and cultural identities undermine collaborative learning. While American colleges and universities now admit diverse people on their way from and to diverse communities, race and ethnicity and gender continue to structure unequal access to and experiences and success in college (Espinosa et al. 2019; Inoue 2015; Museus 2011; Rhoades 2014; Steele 2011). Racism establishes a set of indirect, pliable barriers to the full participation of people of color in American social institutions (Bonilla-Silva 2018). From our perspective, American colleges and universities cannot embrace collaborative learning without confronting racism.

Programs that promote collaborative learning confront racism by design. Spaces designed to promote collaborative learning provide opportunities and support for all participants to pose and pursue questions about their own and others' patterns of learning and solving problems. Collaborative learning happens in spaces in which all participants assume that others—those from minoritized as well as from dominant groups—bring with them potentially promising ideas and productive approaches to problem-solving. Collaborative learners reflect on what and how they learn and how what the network is learning is transforming their identities, practices, and understandings. They come to expect the "blending, merging, meshing dialects" that Vershawn Ashanti Young has described (2009, 72).

Programs that scaffold collaborative learning design spaces that incorporate ongoing dialogue about how participants are interacting, including the ways that some individual and group identities are not being valued and some participants directly or indirectly are being asked to relinquish aspects of their identities and cultural practices in order to participate. In American colleges and universities, this dialogue cannot avoid taking up the ways in which American undergraduate education has required students from some racial and ethnic groups to undergo "enforced educational schizophrenia" (Gilyard 1991, 163), to code-switch, and to manage multiple personalities just to participate (Young 2009). To make spaces for diverse participants to contribute to the learning of all, a curriculum that promotes collaborative learning asks everyone to reflect on and recognize the ways in which mainstream undergraduate education continues to normalize white ways of speaking, listening, acting, reading, writing, thinking, feeling, believing, and valuing.

An education that educates collaborative learners also sets as an educational goal the development of spaces that are *"fairer, more livable, and sustainable for everyone"* (Inoue 2015, 82). Every collaborative learner depends on the contributions of every other learner in the network. Developing spaces—from classes to tutoring centers to offices in which students meet with faculty and staff to "little band practice rooms" where they meet with one another—that sustain all participants is a shared value, and designing and sustaining those spaces is everyone's business. Equitable spaces, Asao Inoue has argued, include formal opportunities for all participants—students, staff, and faculty—to reflect on the conditions and effects of the educational space for individuals, groups, and the community of learners. That reflection calls attention to and makes explicit the norms that govern interaction in the space. This kind of reflection is one of the core practices of collaborative learning. Individually and together, collaborative leaners examine who is participating in the space and who is not, how networks are formed and cultivated and how much power newbies and minoritized people have in the space. Rather than taking success and failure as givens, participants ask how success and failure are constructed and communicated and attributed. Rather than accepting extant knowledge and solutions to problems at face value, they ask about what texts and solutions are circulated, by whom they were produced, and how they are related to the ways in which minoritized participants make meaning and solve problems.

In the following chapters, we explore what we have come to think of as pathways to institutional transformation. Within these pathways we identify and elaborate on diverse programs and practices in which some colleges and universities are embracing and nourishing collaborative learning. In chapter 3, we explore how to cultivate an institutional culture that places collaborative learning as the cornerstone of the undergraduate experience. Chapter 4 takes up the ways in which a shared "commitment to collaboration" blends traditional roles and responsibilities of students, staff, and faculty. Chapters 5 and 6 explore two instructional practices—infusing channels of feedback on problem-solving throughout the curriculum and anchoring the curriculum in shared problem-solving—that engage students, staff, and faculty in sustaining collaboration across the undergraduate experience.

While institutional transformation that incorporates collaborative learning throughout the college experience is a formidable challenge, it is challenge that must be addressed if undergraduate education is to remain relevant in a democracy wrestling with "persistent social inequalities, widening political divisions, prolonged international conflict, and intensifying environmental challenges" (Commission on the Future of Undergraduate Education 2017, v). We believe that undergraduate education can serve as a space in which students, staff, and faculty learn together with local communities to address shared problems and to capitalize on opportunities. A twenty-first century education can become a pathway for students to become collaborative learners who have the capabilities to contribute to shared problem-solving in their workplace, public, and personal lives.

CHAPTER 3

Situating Collaborative Learning at the Center of the Undergraduate Experience

In the networked world of the twenty-first century, American college graduates need to be prepared to connect with others in communities, workplaces, and a multilayered democracy that is negotiating local and global social inequities, political conflicts, and environmental challenges. The word "collaboration" is often woven into institutional missions and statements of student learning outcomes, but what it means for students to collaborate is rarely defined. Moreover, the term often seems to refer not to collaborative learning but to cooperation or teamwork in which individuals mostly divide up roles and responsibilities to solve predefined problems rather than blend roles and responsibilities in shared problem-solving. To flourish and contribute in the worlds they will enter after college, students need to be educated to learn from, with, and for others.

Cultures at most colleges and universities—the norms, values, and beliefs that guide everyday behavior—define college student success in terms of individual achievement. While there are multiple opportunities for teamwork and group work at most institutions, a commitment to learning together is often hard to detect. Situating collaborative learning as the cornerstone of the undergraduate experience requires the cultivation of a campus-wide culture that provides a blueprint to guide students, staff, and faculty with respect to who to be, how to interact with others, and how to go about their everyday lives in college.

In the MSI study, we observed a handful of practices that guide students, faculty, and staff to embrace an alternative to mainstream culture and to place collaboration at the core of the undergraduate experience. In this chapter we piece together what we learned about building an institutional culture anchored in collaborative learning based on our visits to two Minority-Serving Institutions: Paul Quinn College (PQC) and the College of Menominee Nation (CMN). Both of these colleges, as expressed at PQC, emphasize "We over Me." As we looked across programs at PQC and CMN we identified four institutional practices for establishing and sustaining collaborative learning as a centerpiece of a campus-wide culture. These two colleges were reframing undergraduate education as collaborative learning; making explicit and sharing the norms of interdependence and collaboration; expecting students, faculty, and staff to embrace the identity of a collaborative learner; and networking programs and practices with the public and private sectors. These practices were knit into the fabric of these two MSIs, and they have the potential to transform cultures that are grounded in individual learning and competition by valuing and drawing upon the voices, perspectives, and life experiences of all participants. These four practices set the stage for collaborative learning.

Reframe Undergraduate Education
as Collaborative Learning

During our campus visits, leaders at PQC and CMN emphasized that their institutions were disrupting business-as-usual in undergraduate education by embracing a collaborative culture. Driven by shared leadership among administrators and faculty and its identity as a Tribal College, CMN has adopted an approach to undergraduate education that places participation in a community of problem-solvers at the core of the college experience. Since arriving at PQC, President Michael Sorrell has been a transformative leader who has been at the forefront of rescripting the undergraduate experience around collaborative learning.

While neither PQC nor CMN explicitly draws campus-wide attention to the concept of "collaborative learning," both institutions have intentionally framed the undergraduate experience as a developmental process of entering communities and networks where participants are obligated to work interdependently in their learning and problem-solving. As we walked around their campuses and talked with students and staff, we were often told that college was a collective as much as an individual journey: students were responsible for contributing to the learning of their peers and connecting what they were learning to serving their home communities. The commitments to interdependence and to community put collaborative learning—as we came to define it—at the core of their institutional culture. As students, faculty, and staff at PQC put it, a Quinn education comes with the expectation that students take on the identity of a community member in putting "we over me."

We were frequently struck by how both PQC and CMN have explicitly and implicitly put in place an ethos of togetherness.

PQC's mission emphasizes that students are educated to be servant leaders and agents of change in their communities. On its website and through social media feeds and in their admissions and advising practices, the college routinely asks students to rethink the purpose of their education in terms of "greatness": "The Goal is greatness. Greatness for you and those you will serve." Filling out an application and signing up for courses is framed explicitly as choosing "we over me" and joining and contributing to the "Quinnite Nation." Students, staff, and faculty at PQC are expected to view undergraduate education as learning with others to become a nation that will improve their communities. They are all part of what Quinn has named a New Urban College.

The CMN website and outreach materials emphasize that a college education at the CMN campus on the Menominee Reservation and at the nearby urban satellite campus is closely linked to a people and land that includes the "historic Menominee forest." While a growing number of non-Native students are now attending CMN, the mission is unabashedly place-bound. The college was founded, administrators emphasized to us, to educate the next generation of tribal members who "will run things around here." Annual reports highlight that commitment, breaking down the race and ethnicity of students and faculty into "American Indian" and "Other," and disaggregating the tribal affiliation of students. Coursework, the catalog states and staff confirmed, "is infused with American Indian culture." Students we interacted with often spoke about tribal citizenship and home cultures, not only their own but also those of their peers and faculty and staff. This cultural alignment is reflected in public events, celebrations, the names of buildings, and community-centered programs.

In contrast to mainstream culture, with its hierarchies and celebration of individual accomplishments, both PQC and CMN have established cultures that bring individuals together in networks engaged in problem-solving that depend upon the contributions of every participant. Reflecting this collaborative culture, newsfeeds and ceremonies at these two MSIs call out who has contributed and frequently highlight that the institution values and provides spaces in which students, staff, and faculty work together in shared problem-solving that benefits the communities from which students come. This collaborative culture has long been an integral part of the mission of Historically Black Colleges and Universities (HBCUs) and Tribal Colleges and Universities (TCUs), institutions that were designed to provide access to higher education to students who have been excluded and, at the same time, to support their communities not well served by American higher education (Guillory and Ward 2008; Strayhorn and Hirt 2008). In implementing their MSI mission, these colleges recognize and value the cultural heritage of students and link a successful college education to the success of the communities from which students come. In so doing, they strengthen students' connection to college and to their education by inviting them to view their learning in college as closely linked to their embracing long-term responsibility to contribute to the well-being of their home communities (Castellanos and Gloria 2007; Guiffrida 2006). These institutions embrace what Arnetha Ball, Django Paris, and many others call resource pedagogies. They view the identities, literacies, and cultural practices that students bring to school as resources "to honor, explore, and extend" while they encounter the identities, literacies, and practices that are taught and used in school (Paris 2012, 94).

The cultures we observed at CMN, PQC, and the other institutions in the MSIs study rescript conventional participation in undergraduate education. Web pages and orientations to college are infused with multimodal representations of the ways in which students, staff, and faculty take on local issues. Students are represented as learners who are not only expected to ask questions but also to offer responses, and to participate in informal cohorts in which they shuttle among the roles of newbie, tutor, and teacher. The institutional cultures at CMN and PQC value what each stakeholder—including students and their home communities as well as partners in the federal government and the corporate world—brings to the college community, and they establish spaces in which all stakeholders expect to share their perspectives. Group accomplishments are viewed as successful when students, staff, faculty, and external partners have moved forward together in addressing real-world challenges and opportunities that are relevant to the lives of students and their respective communities.

This framing of student success in college explicitly disrupts the dominant emphasis in higher education on autonomy and competition without losing the expectation for individuals to succeed. Some MSIs embrace this commitment because their historic mission demands that they do so (Guillory and Ward, 2008), while others do so mostly because they must in order to serve their students (Laden 2004). The programs in the MSIs study have missions centered on student-centeredness, innovation, and equity—commitments that are an integral part of an institution-wide dedication to collaboration (Kezar 2005). No less important, they embrace and sustain a shared culture that is committed to educating students to be prepared and committed to give back to their communities. They have redefined success in undergraduate education as contributing to success of all students and, in so doing, they are problematizing the dominant emphasis in higher education on individual learning by offering an alternative script. While this script presents a significant challenge to PWIs that have been designed to serve white students, we see the script for undergraduate education that is being developed at PQC and CMN as a way forward. The challenge is to call out the dominant narrative and invite students to see their success as dependent on the success of their peers and the communities that they are preparing to enter.

Make Explicit and Share the Norms of Interdependence and Collaboration

At PQC and CMN, a collaborative culture is rooted in the norms and values that shape the everyday practices and lives of all participants. These norms and values were explicit in the two programs that we studied at the College of Menominee Nation: the STEM Scholars and the STEM Leaders programs. Supported with external funding, these programs were part of a longstanding institutional commitment to produce Native American STEM scholars and leaders who use science and technology to enrich Tribal lands, cultures, and peoples. As emphasized by several administrators at CMN, mainstream higher education too often fails to educate Native American STEM graduates and has fallen short of placing community development and solving local problems as a major emphasis in STEM fields of study.

CMN developed STEM programs in alignment with its core values: serving the community, preserving the environment, and bringing STEM to the Menominee Reservation in ways that align with tribal values. STEM faculty and program staff arranged themselves as networks that support the educational progress of each student in the STEM Scholars and STEM Leaders programs—from their participation in classes and co-curricular activities to public presentations. Students, advisors, faculty, and administrators with whom we spoke at CMN linked the success of students in the STEM programs to the expectations that were set as a condition of entry to the program. "Talking frankly" about student preparation and performance and about the challenges that Native American students had faced at Predominantly White Institutions (PWIs) were knit into cohort meetings and workshops. Talk about academic performance was often addressed by participants in the college community and a local community. That talk could be "frank" for two reasons. First, the programs were designed to serve the communities of the students who enrolled. Program staff knew students and often students' families and Tribes. They understood and spoke about the histories of Native students and respected the traditions and values that shaped the home communities of Native students. Second, staff explicitly rejected "paternalistic attitudes" that framed students as not yet ready to take responsibility for their own education. Students were viewed, as one leader put it, as "adult people." Their progress in classes was tied explicitly to learning about local needs for scientists and to building upon their learning in STEM to work together with community partners and national associations to solve real-world problems. "Dressing the part" and "talking the talk" as a Native American scientist, this leader told us, was both supported and expected.

Interdependence and shared problem-solving were deeply rooted in these programs at CMN. STEM Scholars and Leaders were being educated to bring STEM expertise to the Menominee

Reservation. Courses, faculty emphasized, mirrored those at the flagship PWI in the state so that CMN students were prepared to continue their education at PWIs if they chose to do so. But course practices were also redesigned to educate Native American scientists and technologists. Across the CMN campus, conversations often took place among faculty, students, and community leaders about what it meant for a Native American student to study STEM. These conversations affirmed that every student can learn science and pass classes while also acknowledging that learning and passing STEM courses can be challenging for many students who enroll at CMN. Many students come from high schools with limited resources, and many students manage what Claude Steele (2011) refers to as "stereotype threat"— an awareness of the belief that Indians are not good at STEM and fear of confirming that stereotype.

CMN plugs students into informal and formal networks both on and off campus that encouraged and supported students to view their education as bringing "home" their learning. As an administrator put it: "[F]or the Menominee, to send people out and to learn what was going on beyond their boundaries and then have those people come back is a traditional way of doing things. Up until . . . probably the 1940s, most Menominee families sent someone to Chicago for a while just so they could learn what white people do. . . . That's where they went. And that's a traditional sort of way of doing things for the Menominee." Students at CMN told us about being asked to bring home what they had learned in internships, conferences, and semesters at PWIs, and they often voiced surprise and pleasure at becoming aware that they were part of a network of Native Americans who are learning science, contributing to the success of programs like those at CMN, and doing science at research universities and on the reservation. They came to realize, as one student put it, that "being challenged" was building their capacity to "interpret" STEM for people on their reservation. As this student elaborated: "It's not individually; it's community."

As we learned at CMN, building a collaborative culture that reimagines student success in college requires inviting students, staff, and faculty to learn and practice a nonmainstream set of expectations to guide undergraduate education. Orientations and early experiences invited students, staff, and faculty to come together to reflect on the ways in which mainstream education in the United States values the piling up of personal stores of knowledge and skills—brief forays into group projects notwithstanding. In contrast, the STEM Scholars and Leaders programs at CMN explicitly tethered participation to a commitment to be held responsible for shared endeavors that is no less important than other purposes that students might have brought to college. Access to a college education at CMN comes with a commitment to problem-solving that contributes to the lives of others—peers, staff, and faculty as well as communities surrounding the campus.

The shared norms, values, and behaviors that fueled the STEM programs at CMN support building relationships more than individual achievement. A Native American student we interviewed at CMN described her decision to "stop out" of college several years earlier because the challenges she was facing in her personal life would not allow her to participate fully in the STEM program. She was preparing to "step back in with confidence" that she would be welcomed back into the STEM program. Her peers and CMN staff and faculty, she told us, understood her need to put family ahead of her own education for a time and affirmed her returning to college when she was ready. Program staff repeatedly emphasized to us that they believed in the capacity of every individual to engage others and contribute in their programs. These values at CMN served to guide the ways in which students and institutional staff work together to ensure that every student feels a sense of belonging that validates them as college students.

What we learned from students at CMN and other MSIs has been explored in the well-established body of research on the ways that campus cultures can cultivate a sense of belonging for students of color (Hurtado and Carter 1997; Nuñez 2009; Tierney 1992, 1999). In her study of the transition of Latinx students into college, Nuñez describes a sense of belonging as a kind of social capital that includes a "repertoire of information and behaviors helpful in navigating the educational system," "affective support and encouragement with relationship to schooling," connections to a social network that leads to feelings of reciprocity and trust in the institution, and an obligation to give back (25). Being a student at CMN and PQC means drawing on and using their funds of knowledge to collaborate with others in solving shared problems, including persisting in college.

Researchers have found that students at diverse campuses develop a sense of belonging not so much through adopting the values of a traditional academic and social community but through participating in an "intercultural" network in which no one culture dominates (Tanaka 2003). Participation in a network connects students with faculty and staff who validate their participation—often as cultural agents (Rendón, Jalomo, and Nora 2000)—and also talk candidly about what counts as educational progress. While degrees are important, "belonging" at colleges like CMN and PQC meant becoming committed and more capable of "giving back" to the campus and to the communities that the college serves and from which students come and to which they return.

At PQC and CMN, the script for undergraduate education was not checking off a series of formal and informal opportunities to optimize individual potential. Instead, the curriculum and co-curriculum were branded as opportunities for inquiry into shared problems. Rather than engagement with well-structured problems that certify levels of knowledge and skills, students were expected to take on real-world challenges that they may not be able to solve on their own. Student learning included identifying gaps in their learning and responding with humility, respectfulness, and confidence to fill in those gaps where they exist. While students acknowledged their individual contributions to solving problems, their educational success was measured no less by their capacities to enter into existing networks, find ways to add value, and then carry to their subsequent networks what they learned. Reimagining student success as learning from, with, and for others is rooted in these norms. Programs at CMN and PQC suggest a path toward adopting nontraditional norms and values: educational programs that define success in terms of interdependence and call students' attention to the norms and values that make interdependent action/learning possible.

Expect Students, Faculty, and Staff to Embrace the Identity of a Collaborative Learner

Establishing a nontraditional institutional blueprint for undergraduate education requires that students, faculty, and staff try on a nontraditional identity: a collaborative learner. The STEM programs at CMN provided opportunities to practice being the kinds of learners and teachers that this blueprint calls for. The point of entry to these programs incorporated not only high school transcripts and placement scores but also interviews with students. These interviews gathered information not only about students' backgrounds in mathematics and science but also about their commitment to a STEM education. These programs have made placement an opportunity for students to reflect on the purpose of a STEM education.

From the outset, courses and meetings in these STEM programs networked students, program mentors, faculty and, in the case of the STEM Leaders program, an advisory group of faculty, scientists, and Elders. As program participants, students were invited to "present" their own learning to their network, at first in structured opportunities to learn from and with other participants and then in presentations in the community and at regional and national conferences and in internships far from the reservation. Staff and faculty in the network met with students and with one another to share information about student progress and redesign meetings and even class schedules so that students would develop trust in their own "gifts" and "skill sets" and bring those gifts and skill sets to the program. That work, participants emphasized, involves moving the cohort through college—from completing assignments and meeting deadlines to filling out financial aid forms—and "getting out there" in community events and conferences and through internships. One Leader described the ways in which a summer internship in a lab at a Predominantly White Institution helped her believe that she could, "if she wanted to," move on to join new STEM networks.

PQC's New Urban College Model invited students to an undergraduate education structured around "the ideals of disciplined work, servant leadership, and initiative in preparation for lives of financial freedom, community engagement, and outstanding character." From matriculation to graduation and beyond, students were expected to

- Leave places better than you found them
- Lead from wherever you are
- Live a life that matters
- Love something greater than yourself.

A student at Paul Quinn College described her experience as a "revolution and evolution": courses and the co-curriculum reframed education from completing classes to building the capacity to "change the world" with her peers—including finding "answers for their own communities" as one staff member put it. This student cherished her educational experiences at PQC because the college provided structured opportunities for her to reconsider her own beliefs about how to pursue a college education and what that education was for. She talked about being intimidated by the expectation that she would find an internship with a major corporation and then discovering that she had something to offer.

We see in Paul Quinn College and the College of Menominee Nation a template for developing collaborative learners by establishing an environment in which students feel that their cultural identities, values, and experiences have something to offer. Students were invited to see "congruity" between their identities and the identities of those who contribute to the learning of others (Castellanos and Gloria 2007; Gloria and Castellanos 2003; Gloria and Robinson-Kurpius 1996). Both PQC and CMN aimed to disrupt the dominant script in undergraduate education that is grounded in individual learning and competition and, in so doing, redefine undergraduate education in large measure as collaboration among students, faculty, and staff. The backgrounds and communities of students were acknowledged in the curriculum, and across their lived experiences on campus students had a range of opportunities to connect with others. Students came to see themselves and their peers as sources of support. In coming to know and value students and the experiences that they bring to college, faculty and staff joined together in a collective enterprise. Faculty and staff curated educational materials and services that were relevant to their students. Students, staff, and faculty engaged the local community and other regional and national partners. All stakeholders came to see themselves as contributing participants in networks of problem-solvers who take up challenges facing the communities that the colleges serve.

This kind of cultural congruity emerges in undergraduate education as institutions create opportunities for students, staff, and faculty to try out new ways of experiencing college. This script for undergraduate education positions students as members of a network, beginning with their first interactions on campus, and it rewrites conventional course curricula and teaching practices by providing students with opportunities to understand what it means to collaborate. The education of students unfolds in a series of opportunities for scaffolded engagement in collaborative inquiry beginning with their orientation to college. Program requirements—from college strategies courses, first-year interest groups, and required first-year courses to capstone projects and undergraduate research—and the content of required courses are reimagined. Opportunities for collaborative learning are closely linked to opportunities for students to reflect on how they have engaged in collaboration and the ways in which their learning with others has had an impact on their own learning and development, the real-world problems they wish to pursue, and their understanding of the purpose of a college education.

Faculty and staff, as well as students, are expected to embrace and practice the identity of a collaborative learner. Advising sessions and courses are explicitly framed as engagement in ongoing back-and-forth undertakings and include periodic requirements in which students and staff step away to reflect on their involvement and contributions and then share their reflections with others. Speakers and events are sometimes introduced as the result of collaboration and come with the expectation that all participants—presenters and audience members alike—will consider and share the ways in which an event has an impact on ways that real-world problems can be solved.

Approaching college as a collaborative learner who is engaged in local issues through shared problem-solving is a departure from tradition at most institutions—and not only for students. Institutions that take this approach invite all participants to try out the role and identity of a collaborative learner. CMN and PQC explicitly called attention to the roles and responsibilities of students, staff, and faculty. They asked everyone in the entire educational community to embrace the identity of a collaborative learner, and they provide opportunities for everyone to practice learning together as they move forward in addressing real-world challenges and opportunities. These opportunities as CMN and PQC often set students, faculty, and staff on the path to participating in public discussions of local environmental issues that, at PQC, included blocking the location of a proposed landfill. CMN students often became community educators in schools on the reservation.

Network Programs with Local Communities

Given the linkage between collaborative learning and solving real-world problems, institutions that design undergraduate education to include space for collaborative learning find ways to connect student learning to the worlds in which the campus sits. These institutions will likely continue to make use of "high-impact" practices such as study abroad, service-learning, undergraduate research, and other programs that draw undergraduates out of traditional classrooms. The challenge—one taken on by the programs we studied at PQC and CMN—is to go beyond low-incidence, high-impact practices and embed student engagement with the world off campus into the values, norms, and everyday routines of students, staff, and faculty.

Both PQC and CMN positioned education as a space that connects students' home communities to their futures. President Michael Sorrell at PQC visited the homes of students to meet with family members and discuss the college experience, such as opportunities for internships and community engagement and the campus-wide dress code that encouraged students to see themselves as graduates. Under President Sorrell's leadership, the college has emphasized that service to the college and the local community is an integral part of the script. A student we met on campus recalled asking an administrator whether the college would support the development of a dance team, and subsequently being asked to start one. Reflecting on this experience, she described coming to the realization that PQC challenged her beliefs about education. While she had long assumed that the college would make experiences available to her only on campus, she early discovered that being a Paul Quinn student meant taking responsibility on and off campus along with pursuing her own dreams.

STEM programs at the College of Menominee Nation invited students to pursue solutions to challenges facing Native American communities as a driving reason for enrolling in college, and CMN connected students with tribal leaders and working scientists early in their college experience. Students at CMN talked about hearing that they would be participating in community initiatives, national conferences, and internships. Faculty and staff, one student told us, "didn't really give us a choice." Getting a degree meant contributing to networks that were at work on solving real-world problems. Meeting with program staff—from advisors to tutors to mentors—was not optional for STEM students at PQC. Staff at CMN and PQC told us that the purpose of intrusive advising was both to check in on students' academic progress and to discuss with them their purpose for being in college. At PQC, students were challenged to express who they were preparing to serve. STEM Leaders at CMN told us about being required to prepare applications for internships, for transfer to four-year colleges, and even to graduate school.

In addition to embedding participation in real-world problem-solving on campus, both CMN and PQC made moving off campus to learn collaboratively an expectation for students. STEM Leaders at CMN met regularly with Tribal Elders and the scientists who managed the tribal forest and other community resources. Students were, as one CMN STEM Leader put it, "sent" to conferences far from the reservation where they interacted with Native Americans from across the country who were studying science. On returning to campus after one such conference, STEM Leaders established a chapter of the American Indian

Science and Engineering Society and sought grant funding for community projects. At Paul Quinn College students described studying local problems in their business and communication courses and then being sent off campus to study problems like the local "food desert" or a proposed landfill. In so doing, they contacted and met with local government and private funders first to advocate for policies and then to help plan and implement a community farm, make presentations at city council meetings, and participate in a march. As one PQC student told us, the expectation to contribute off campus is an integral part of completing a degree. In listening to stories like this, we became aware that engaging in networks was not an activity initially pursued by many students. It was part of the script for undergraduate education that PQC and CMN were rewriting.

Networking students with off-campus communities has been found by many scholars to be an important part of campus cultures that welcome minority students (Castellanos and Gloria 2007; Kiyama, Museus, and Vega 2015; Museus 2014). Castellanos and Gloria (2007) emphasize that the success of all students is tied to their "sense of efficacy as contributing members of their fields" and that the educational experiences of underrepresented students at mainstream colleges and universities are often disconnected from their home communities (392). As these scholars have emphasized, students are motivated to engage in their own education when they have opportunities to see themselves as contributing to communities. As they participate in undergraduate research and in professional organizations, visit labs and local businesses, and complete internships, they come to believe that they belong on campus.

The institutions in the MSI study suggest a path to engaging local communities; they went beyond building a sense of efficacy to engaging students in shared problem-solving that addressed local problems. This commitment requires, senior leaders emphasized, a willingness to rebrand undergraduate education for students and staff alike. CMN and PQC, for example, provided students with access to and connections with the communities that they serve and prepared students to contribute in those communities through shared problem-solving. Both institutions define a commitment to solving local problems as a cornerstone of the undergraduate experience. They were, in the words of a STEM Leader at CMN, rescripting student success as a community affair: "If the community is successful, you're successful. So we, as STEM Leaders, we're a community. So if one was having trouble, we were all having trouble, so we'd try to help to help that one out." The "one having trouble," he explained, could be a peer in the program, his local community, or the field of sustainability. The challenge he articulates for higher education, especially for PWIs, is to regard contributing to the flourishing of local communities as critical to student success rather than simply something an individual does on their way to a degree.

Conclusion: Toward Cultural Congruity for All Students

An institutional culture—the normative and social glue that can hold an institution together—shapes who students, staff, and faculty believe they can be and what they believe they can do in undergraduate education. The culture at most colleges and universities encourages undergraduate students to find ways to connect who they are and what they hope to do with who they are supposed to be and what they are supposed to do in college. Failing to do so makes departure from college more likely (Tinto 1993). This culture has operated at a time when an undergraduate education marked a common identity and set of experiences that certified individual learners as graduates. We believe that this culture cannot meet the needs of our diverse nation. Why not? First, the diverse students now arriving on college campuses no longer seek a common identity. Cultures designed primarily to assimilate individuals into preexisting institutional cultures often put at a disadvantage whole groups of students— particularly those from communities with collectivist visions of student success and those for whom adopting the identity of college student means relinquishing off-campus identities and experiences. Second, American undergraduate education needs to prepare students to take on shared problems in a complex and often divided democracy. Successful graduates will be prepared to see diversity of experiences and goals as normative and as an asset.

The cultures of many colleges and universities will need to be transformed if American higher education is to provide opportunities for all students to contribute to framing and solving problems in our diverse nation and world (Conrad and Dunek 2020). Most of our colleges and universities remain places that educate self-sufficient learners rather than places that cultivate and sustain networks of diverse individuals engaged in shared problem-solving. As research on the experiences of minority college students confirms, institutional cultures at many PWIs complicate the process of making connections with people and practices that can open up opportunities to learn from and with others, including the growing number of first-generation students and students of color.

For far too long, collegiate cultures have often left finding a way to belong on campus up to students. To address this gap there have been calls for reform that point to the interdependent and collaborative culture that we observed at PQC and CMN (Conrad and Gasman 2015; Guiffrida 2006; Hurtado, Milem, and Clayton-Pedersen 1999; Rendón, Jalomo, and Nora 2000; Tierney 1992; 1999). Through interviewing and surveying students, staff, and faculty, researchers have identified practices that ground a culture in which all students–especially minority students—can connect and contribute as whole people (Castellanos and Gloria 2007; Hurtado, Milem, and Clayton-Pedersen 1999; Kiyama, Museus, and Vega 2015; Museus 2011).

CMN and PQC have adopted practices that do more than connect students to their institutions. They have used these practices to establish the kind of environment that is needed to promote collaborative learning. As emphasized in these institutions, collaborative learning takes place in networks of people who share a real-world, situated challenge and come to that endeavor with varying experiences and perspectives. Engaging in collaborative learning means being an active participant, respectfully engaging others with trust and respect for differences along with the commitment to solving the problem that is being addressed. Collaborative learning as we envision it is structured to invite back-and-forth dialogue and calls attention to and problematizes mainstream dynamics with respect to who may speak, what may be said, what gets in the way of communication, and what contributes to it. Collaborative learning creates spaces in which all participants are invested in learning from, with, and for others.

To engage in collaborative learning, students, staff, and faculty draw on and contribute based on their off-campus identities and experiences as they engage with others in shared problem-solving. To that end, they need campus cultures that validate the diverse cultural capital that each participant brings and invite all participants to draw on their cultural capital as they learn together. Institutions invested in advancing collaborative learning provide cultural congruity for every student and every staff and faculty member and, in so doing, provide every student with opportunities and the obligation to connect with other members of the campus community through community-based learning and internships without surrendering their own identities and experiences. Traveling this path entails explicitly putting an institution in the service of communities and students and then educating students to serve those communities in concert with recognizing and sustaining networks that address real-world problems.

CHAPTER 4

Blending Roles and Responsibilities of Faculty, Staff, and Students

Irrespective of institutional mission, everyday life in undergraduate education at most institutions is structured around longstanding roles and responsibilities—a widely accepted division of labor. The conventional division of labor is structured to deemphasize collaboration. Faculty are experts in their field of study who teach. Students take classes, get grades, and learn what faculty teach. Staff provide support services that supplement classroom instruction, course completion, and the learning of students. Everyone has a lane. In contrast, collaborative learning calls on students, faculty, staff, and administrators to participate in interdependent networks that blend traditional roles and responsibilities. Putting collaborative learning at the center of the undergraduate experience means reframing who students, staff, and faculty expect to be and what they expect to do.

At Salish Kootenai College (SKC) we encountered an institution that has reframed undergraduate education to a large extent as a collective endeavor. This reframing was particularly evident in the Department of Academic Success (DAS), a program developed to support underprepared students along their pathway into and through college. Rather than a traditional academic department housing a set of experts from whom students acquire disciplinary knowledge and expertise, the DAS was designed to be an educational hub—a network of programs that support student success. Regardless of their primary role on campus, everyone in the DAS is engaged in "reinforcing" practices that promote student learning and persistence and, in so doing, connecting students to their education. While the DAS emphasizes the importance of disciplinary knowledge and skills, students and staff and faculty in this department view undergraduate education as "more than academics." Disciplinary knowledge and skills are closely linked to taking on problems shared by families, communities, and the Tribe as well as building the capacity to serve and work on Tribal lands.

Roles and responsibilities in the DAS are fluid. Rather than using positional authority to define relationships, DAS faculty and staff participate in DAS "as themselves"—people with their own experiences, tribal affiliations, and aspirations. What staff and faculty do and are expected to do is rooted in what they know about who students are and where they come from as well as what will support and what will hinder their educational progress. Regardless of their home department, staff and faculty associated with the DAS are expected to learn about financial aid, scholarships, and policies related to formal academic warnings. While the program acknowledges and values the expertise of faculty and staff, participants described learning how to relinquish their authority over students' progress and to genuinely listen to students and colleagues. Several faculty members described discovering that they needed to respect students' need for silence and, at times, space to work out for themselves how to succeed in college. While DAS students, staff, and faculty regularly play different roles, all are expected to listen to, respect, and learn from the ideas advanced by others.

This nontraditional division of labor in the DAS elevates the place of interdependency as students, staff, and faculty come to appreciate that expertise is often distributed across traditional roles and responsibilities. During our visit, faculty recognized that staff sometimes knew more than they did about engaging students with academic content and motivating students. Everyone acknowledged an obligation to build their expertise across DAS activities. Math faculty were learning how to teach reading and mentor students; staff were learning how to design credit-bearing courses; and students were learning how to teach and advise one another and, at times, faculty and staff. As one student put it, he was learning to see himself as "intelligent": "I never saw myself as intelligent, but I know [now] that I am." This student spoke openly about facing his fear of criticism and trading the passive role that he had learned to play in school for an active one that obligated him to take the initiative to occasionally teach and advise his peers and even staff and faculty.

A Tribal College by mission and identity, Salish Kootenai College broke away from the traditional division of labor in undergraduate education by leveraging institutional commitments to the success of underprepared students and service to local communities. Students, staff, and faculty were will willing to blend roles and responsibilities and arrived at a division of labor that established the foundation for collaborative learning. In this chapter, we highlight three practices that facilitate the blending of traditional roles and responsibilities: co-teaching, distributing responsibility for student progress, and creating research opportunities for students and faculty.

Co-Teach

The study of Minority-Serving Institutions pointed us to the potential of blurring the role of teacher. Across many of the programs at the twelve MSIs, faculty shared the task of teaching with other faculty, students, and staff. Initiatives in the MSIs included formal Peer Led Team Learning, Supplemental Instruction, learning communities, peer mentoring and advising, and informal collaboration between tutoring centers and faculty. Students, staff, and faculty talked about how much they appreciated two teachers being in the same classroom. They described staff and near peers—students who had recently completed the course—teaching courses that supplemented courses taught by faculty, near peers and peers leading study sessions that reflected on the material covered in credit-bearing courses, and even students teaching modules in their own courses from time to time. Administrators told us about managing budgets, faculty loads, and contracts to make such distribution of teaching possible.

The MSIs were leveraging a well-established practice. Co-teaching has long been used at colleges and universities to make general education accessible to special populations as well as to provide interdisciplinary experiences for students and professional development for faculty. Defined as "some level of collaboration in the planning and delivery of a course" (Davis, 1995), co-teaching is a diverse practice. It includes courses team-taught by two or more faculty who are always in the room, courses taught sequentially by different teachers, and courses in which students or staff members teach different segments during a class session. By definition, the practice leads to reexamining disciplinary boundaries and content (Harris and Harvey 2000) and developing relationships among co-teachers (Dunn and Wallace 2008; Spencer-Oatey 2013). The multiplication of teachers almost always changes interactions between teachers and students as students adapt to multiple approaches to teaching.

It is important to note that those who adopt the practice of co-teaching may choose to use a traditional, cooperative division of labor: dividing up responsibilities based on expertise and positional roles. This approach often appears to set faculty scrambling as they negotiate ownership of a classroom and to frustrate students as they negotiate two styles of teaching and approaches to grading (Jones and Harris 2012; Morelock et al. 2017). Alternatively, co-teaching can embed collaboration into the structure of educational experiences, transforming teachers into co-constructors of knowledge and students "from passive recipients of information given by an expert teacher to active agents in the construction of knowledge" (Goodsell et al. 1992). As Eisen (2000) expressed this, "the practice of sharing power with co-teachers paves the way for sharing control with learners" (7).

Publications on co-teaching provide numerous examples of sharing of control. Robert Nash (2009) described the "crossover pedagogy" that he developed across years of team teaching with student affairs professionals in a professional school at the University of Vermont. At Antioch University in Seattle, Candace Harris and Anne Harvey (2000) developed a two-quarter learning community to model a process of learning and interacting in the bachelor's degree completion program. The design of the course defines faculty as both learners and teachers as they develop a curriculum and share instruction with a colleague and ultimately with students. Students observe faculty members making sense of content as relative novices and negotiating their understanding of content with one another. The design, for

Harris and Harvey, creates an opportunity to foster collaboration: "In a context where we are also trying to challenge the Western norm of individual learning, one of our intentions is to build collaborative skills and awareness of collective responsibility. We emphasize that each member of the learning community has a responsibility to contribute to constructing new knowledge. Seeing us demonstrate these skills gives the students a model of how to increase their own collaborative skills." (30)

At Eastern Michigan University and the University of Michigan, a group of English faculty borrowed the method of *hevruta* from yeshivas to displace the traditional teacher-student relationship (Bergom et al. 2011). As undergraduates take up this method, they engage in a semester-long conversation with a partner they select at the beginning of the term. Together, these peers grapple with the course content; brief written reflections are sent to partners and the instructor at the same time; and final exams are taken by groups of four to six students. Surveys and focus groups document a shift in the way many students view learning: it becomes "contextual and relative." Completing the class involves taking the time to listen to others—peers as well as instructors—and to question assumptions and first readings as well as relying on interactions with others to deepen their understanding.

At the University of Calgary, a senior-level nursing class is routinely team-taught. Students observe nursing faculty—who are also nurses—interact professionally. As the course unfolds, students collaborate in designing a health education session, co-teaching a nursing laboratory session for junior nursing students, and writing a formal reflection on the impact of co-teaching on their understanding of health education (Lock et al. 2018).

Tisdell and Eisen (2000) describe what cuts across these examples of co-teaching: co-teaching establishes an educational environment that is different from business-as-usual in undergraduate education. Whatever the makeup of a co-taught class, it is not a disciplinary expert transmitting information to students. In disrupting the traditional division of labor, teachers and students engaged in co-teaching are obligated to position themselves intentionally in relationship to course content. Nash (2009) emphasizes that co-teaching often leads to organizing courses around local challenges that students, staff, and faculty share rather than around a predefined block of disciplinary content. Harris and Harvey (2000) describe "joint construction of a course" as changing the way that it is conventionally designed. Across the examples discussed above, collaboration anchors the course in a shared endeavor among faculty and staff and students as well.

The design of a co-taught course also initiates an ongoing process of negotiating relationships and activities. Faculty and students are faced with decisions about how to share power with one another and how to interact when there is not one teacher to please and students are also someone else's students. Co-teachers describe various ways in which being a co-teacher often draws them out as learners who have experiences that frame their approach to problem-solving. Faced with co-designed inquiry into a shared problem, students must make sense of diverse perspectives and often different approaches to the endeavor as they observe faculty members dialogue and peers teach and learn in the classroom. In turn, they decide how to position themselves in a dialogue. After participating in *hevruta* or in a co-taught nursing course, students often describe realizing that they have to trust that other participants, regardless of their positional role, are contributing to a shared endeavor. Students learn to listen to a range of perspectives and strengthen their abilities to both take apart and synthesize diverse ideas and, in so doing, strengthen their critical thinking skills. As Harris and Harvey (2000, 29) put it: "Diversity is experienced as being valuable." Getting better at collaborating with diverse others becomes an explicit goal for all participants.

As Tisdale and Eisen (2000) emphasize, the instructional practice of co-teaching brings knowledge construction and problem-solving to the fore and pushes the acquisition of required content to the background. Across the examples discussed here, faculty recognize the need to collaborate in making sense of the course topic. Students appear to as well. Students observe disciplinary experts making sense of other people's ideas with respect to a shared problem. The central activity in the classroom moves from the explication of content by an expert to the active process of framing and solving problems across differences, opening up space for all participants to embrace the uncertainty and risk at the heart of learning and to feel a responsibility for engaging others in the pursuit of promising ideas.

Co-teaching has great potential to disrupt the traditional division of labor. It also can establish a foundation for collaborative learning. Many of the faculty we met in the MSI study found that sharing the role of teaching has led them to embrace the role of "learner" among "learners." Some faculty described sharing content coverage and focusing more on strategies for learning and using "their" content. Not only did faculty team up, but peers and near peers often met with students before, during, and after scheduled classes. A San Diego City College (SDCC) math teacher, for instance, described watching a Supplemental Instruction leader explain course material and strategies for completing assignments in ways she would not. When she stepped back in as teacher, she acknowledged this approach and added her own. Passing the responsibility of teaching to a back-and-forth with a novice made her anxious, yet at the same time she acknowledged that this novice connected with students differently and, she mused, kept them engaged with the problem at hand and helped them stay engaged in completing a college math requirement.

For students in the MSIs study, co-teaching means having "more voices" explaining course material and thus more opportunities to hear content represented or problems solved differently. This makes it more likely, a SDCC student explained, that she would have course work represented in a "way that made sense to me." Hearing more voices had an additional impact. While this student admitted she had a tendency to be an individual learner seeking A's, talking with faculty, tutors, and peers made her begin to suspect that A's represented the outcomes of her participation in a network. She explained that she was starting to accept that getting A's meant offering her ideas and hearing those of others. Learning was more than just picking up points on assignments and tests. Success in a first-year writing course, she admitted, was not figuring out what the teacher wanted but engaging in the work of the class, hearing how her writing affected others, and communicating clearly.

Still another impact that students in the MSI study mentioned almost in passing was motivation. The blending of traditional teaching roles meant that they encountered more people who were intentionally invested in their success. Students identified by name advisors and fellow students as teachers who seemed close to students' immediate educational experience and aware of the ways in which students were succeeding and struggling. More teachers meant that there were more people that students did not want to let down and more points of contact that kept students engaged in moving forward in a course.

Co-teaching shifts the classroom endeavor from satisfying a teacher to engaging in spirited dialogue in which sometimes a teacher, sometimes a student, and sometimes a staff member pushes the process forward. Everyone is obligated to engage in the dialogue and to respect what others bring to the ongoing conversation. This practice is a path to institutional transformation in part because it calls attention to traditional roles and intentionally shifts power from one set of role players to others. It opens the possibility of new voices, previously ignored voices, re-framing issues and problems, and offering new ideas and solutions. It is a practical way to disrupt the division of labor in higher education.

Distribute Responsibility for Student Progress

The idea that student progress should be the responsibility of the entire institution is not new. Beginning near the end of World War II, student support services were greatly expanded in response to the broadening of access to college through the GI Bill and the Higher Education Act. Opening access meant, among other things, developing opportunities for precollege academic development, and assisting students who enroll to meet basic college requirements along with motivating and guiding students to attain their educational goals. Support services have been critical in expanding access to higher education, and yet the idea has been incompletely realized in mainstream higher education. Notwithstanding the contributions of student support services, Bailey, Jaggars, and Jenkins (2015) found in their review of student support services at community colleges 50 years after the Higher Education Act that student support services have limited impact when they "merely provide information, without teaching students how to correctly and effectively apply that information in different contexts across time" (67). These services, they observed, are rarely integrated with students' programs of study.

Most student support services in our nation's colleges and universities reinforce the traditional division of labor in higher education. Staff offer information and advice to support students in their journey through college, and innovations that disrupt this division of labor sit on the edges of the undergraduate experience. Alignment between high school and undergraduate education remains a work in progress: meetings with advisors and tutors are optional and usually brief, instrumental exchanges; college success courses and faculty professional development are disconnected from the rest of the curriculum; and tutoring and Supplemental Instruction programs are not often used as they are frequently stigmatized.

The fix? *Redesigning American Community Colleges* (Bailey, Jaggars, and Jenkins 2015) lays out a plan for providing students with information to develop and pursue their educational goals through a robust case management system. It calls on colleges to establish crossfunctional teams of staff and faculty who work with students to establish and document educational goals, build educational plans, track progress, and provide help when and where it is needed. While we see much promise in this vision of support services, it remains primarily focused on moving individual learners to degrees. Rescripting an institution as a place where students, staff, and faculty work together will require breaking down traditional roles and distributing responsibility for student progress. Students need to be invited into the role of contributor; faculty members, that of learners about student success; advisors, that of instructional designers and teachers. Rather than a resource for students who are not adequately prepared to complete college degree programs, we suggest that student support services should become an integral part of everyday life in which every member of the educational community views supporting student progress as a shared responsibility.

Bailey, Jaggers, and Jenkins (2015) point to colleges providing this kind of support. We observed this kind of student support in the twelve institutions in the MSI study. Most of these institutions had established crossfunctional teams of staff and faculty to review and support the progress of students in programs. Support services were intrusive, required, and challenged conventional routines of students, staff, and faculty, and this support was designed and delivered by peers, staff, and faculty in various ways. The MSIs were directly and indirectly drawing on an integration of support services that has been mapped out for decades by researchers who have explored the success of racial and ethnic minorities and other underrepresented students (Attinasi 1989; Hurtado, Milem, and Clayton-Pedersen 1999; Markus and Kitayama 1991; Museus 2011; Pizzolato et al. 2012; Rendón, Jalomo, and Nora 2000; Torres 2006). Colleges and universities invested in the success of all students in a diverse student body place the experiences of students who have traditionally been poorly served by American higher education at the center of conversations about student success and pursue institutional cultures and practices that these students find supportive. They aim for what Samuel Museus and colleagues have described as "culturally engaging campus environments" (CECE). The CECE model identifies educational practices—what

Museus and associates call "cultural characteristics"—that have been found to promote the success of minoritized students (Kiyama, Museus, and Vega 2015; Museus 2011; Museus and Ravello 2010). We see in the CECE model a set of student support practices that rework the roles that students, staff, and faculty are expected to play and establish the conditions for collaborative learning.

Foremost, culturally engaging support is "proactive" and adds to the role of every program participant the responsibility to contribute to the success of all students. Rather than simply passing along information about opportunities for development, assistance, or guidance for which they are responsible, staff and faculty expect to do what a staff member we interviewed at North Seattle College called "walkovers" and "huddles." When a student is faced with a need for support, staff members physically connect them with sources of support on campus or huddle up with other staff members to determine what source of support would likely meet their need and then walk the student over. The central role, for example, of a financial aid advisor is not simply to gather financial information and ask for forms to be completed on time—though following policy is important. Rather, their role is one of a proactive problem-solver who is engaged with helping to ensure that a student can complete the next step in their education. If that next step is connecting with an advisor or a tutor in addition to squaring away funding, financial aid staff walk the student to the sources of support they need. As Museus and associates found, a commitment to keeping students participating in their own education means committing resources—personnel, programs, and financial support—to relevant sources of support and developing a staff network that connects students to support through relationships. As working together across units to ensure that students will continue to pursue their education becomes part of the formal and informal job description of staff and faculty, students come to see college as a space designed to keep them engaged in learning.

Institutions that provide proactive services that are culturally engaging establish networks of staff and faculty who know and value students and one another. We see in the holistic practices and family networks that are part of a culturally engaging campus a distributed system that respects and makes space for diverse personal and cultural backgrounds and obligates members to contribute based on their knowledge, skills, and the experiences they bring to college. Museus and Ravello (2010) found that academic advising at a culturally engaging campus involves participants expecting to take up students' needs together, dialoguing about solutions without reducing those needs to the services offered by a single program or resource. Staff step into the role of action researcher who is curious about students' academic, social, and psychological challenges and sees them as interrelated. Interacting with one member of a student support network leads students into interactions with others.

Closely tethered to an ethos of interdependence, culturally engaging student support practices are "humanized" practices— practices taken up by human beings with experiences and histories and cultures who respect and care about the experiences, histories, and cultures of those with whom they interact. Through hiring practices to professional development, staff and faculty are invited to share their experiences along with their professional judgments and strategies. Students at the MSI Models campuses often emphasized that staff and faculty identified challenges they had faced as college students. At El Paso Community College, for example, two students reflected on the impact of their knowing that an advisor also had to learn English while completing college courses that were taught in English. That advisor become a source of inspiration, a trusted source of information, and a person not to let down. Interacting with her led these students to approach their education differently. As they talked with an advisor who understood their paths, they began to take advantage of advising and tutoring programs, retook placement tests to increase their odds for getting into programs, took courses in sequences that supported their language learning, and pursued scholarships set aside for working Latinas seeking health care and business degrees. This "humanized support" drew them into a student support network, deepening their engagement with their education and leading to more creative solutions to the challenges they were facing. As importantly, the people in the humanized support network learned to question standard practices. A humanized network of support can provide a safe space for students to express their needs and to find and draw on resources that matter to them.

Finally, culturally engaging student support makes using support services mandatory. Museus and colleagues observed this at institutions that were effective in promoting minority student success. We also observed this in the MSIs study. As an EPCC administrator mused: "Students don't do optional; hell, I don't do optional." An SDCC leader described support services as tethering participation in the First-Year Experience program with participating in a series of "required" activities—from learning about financial aid to visiting transfer schools to meeting with advisors. Staff and faculty at SDCC felt that checking in with students concerning their use of support was expected, and they described a sense of obligation to work with students and others to resolve challenges that had little to do with their primary role as a teacher or advisor. The institution becomes responsible for the success of every student, especially students who have traditionally been poorly served. Support becomes collaboration and supports collaborative learning. Student development, support, and guidance is an endeavor that is shared among diverse staff members on campus whose roles are continually redefined by their relationships with the students they serve. The responsibility to develop "whole students"—students who are empowered to contribute by drawing on their knowledge, experiences, and cultures—is distributed across the campus community.

Culturally engaging support services make student development, support, and guidance the responsibility of the entire campus. Support becomes an integral part of undergraduate education. Many administrators in the MSIs study described repositioning faculty and staff members and restructuring support programs so that faculty and staff members were not just role players in the spaces through which students moved. At SDCC, faculty talked about holding back on course content until they had a chance to talk about college expectations. At North Seattle College, a staff member explained that support services were useful to the extent that the college was able "to integrate social, educational, and employment services." For her, education was a "social service." In the Department of Academic Success at Salish Kootenai College, faculty and staff and peers are expected to step into support roles. Students, staff, and faculty are all obligated to keep students moving forward. Student success is, at once, a challenge and an opportunity that everyone takes up rather than focusing exclusively on the tasks assigned in the traditional division of labor. As roles blur, educational opportunities and institutions are transformed.

Create Research Opportunities for Students and Faculty

Most of the programs in the study of Minority-Serving Institutions included opportunities for students to be researchers as well as students (Conrad and Gasman 2015). Students at Morehouse College and SKC published papers and traveled to conferences. One of the program requirements for STEM Leaders at the College of Menominee Nation was a research internship. Drawing on a well-established educational strategy (Auchincloss et al. 2014; Buck, Bretz, and Towns 2008; Lopatto 2003; Weaver, Russell, and Wink 2008), these institutions created programs to provide students with a range of opportunities to engage in research, especially putting students in teams engaged in an iterative process to address research questions relevant to worlds beyond the classroom. Students described reading relevant literature, being involved in research design, and taking on responsibility for communicating results. Without exception, they emphasized that these programs required them to collaborate with others.

Program administrators in the MSIs study described the value of these undergraduate research programs in terms very similar to those laid out in the Boyer Commission Report (1998) and in the mission of the Council on Undergraduate Research (https://www.cur.org/who/organization/mission/). These administrators believed that providing students with opportunities to be researchers connected them with faculty mentors and deepened their connections to their program of study, their peers, and their institution. Students emphasized that they learned how research is done and enhanced their research skills, and many emphasized their learning how to talk with others about their research and in some cases how to contribute to research being conducted by a local department of natural resources or, in one case, a NASA lab. Students often spoke—with some surprise—about developing identities as researchers with a commitment to engage in local problem-solving.

While the MSIs study confirmed a plethora of research on the value of undergraduate research (Eagan et al. 2013; Hunter et al. 2009; Hurtado et al. 2008; Schultz et al. 2011), we became interested in how these programs—course-based undergraduate research and apprenticeship-based undergraduate research initiatives—were blurring the roles of students, staff, and faculty by making explicit the norms that define different roles, altering student-faculty relationships, and adding in off-campus communities as active program participants (Bangera and Brownell 2014). This blurring, we came to appreciate, has great potential to reposition students, staff, and faculty as collaborative learners.

Consider the undergraduate research opportunities at Beloit College, a liberal arts college in Wisconsin. Undergraduate students conduct research across the curriculum in part because undergraduate education at Beloit College is defined as "the liberal arts in practice." Beloit College is committed to supporting students in engaging in "inquiry or investigation . . . that makes an original intellectual or creative contribution." Opportunities for students to develop research skills figures prominently in the college's strategic plan, and that commitment finds expression in a student research symposium and opportunities in departments across the curriculum for course-based research. Degree requirements include a capstone and a "'beyond the classroom' liberal arts in practice experience." The college has gathered significant support for apprentice-based research in the Liberal Arts Practice Center (LAPC). Through the LAPC, students pursue funding for experiential learning projects and apply for undergraduate research internships and programs.

The commitment at Beloit College to provide students with extracurricular opportunities for personal professional development could be met by students, staff, and faculty without challenging the traditional division of labor in undergraduate education. No blurring required. Yet, one of the programs at Beloit College, the Sanger Summer Research Program, suggests the potential for undergraduate research to build on more than the contribution of an individual. The program seems to force blurring. Student participation comes with a work requirement— participants cannot work off campus—that turns students temporarily into employees of the college who are expected to be on campus during the entire program. Rather than simply joining a lab or project, students develop with program faculty a "collaborative model" that describes what they will do together, even if that involves participating in an ongoing project. Throughout the summer, students and faculty meet weekly with a "research cluster" of other Sanger teams and routinely participate in program meetings. In effect, program faculty become de facto staff who schedule meetings, advise, and manage logistics as well as inquirers who explore other people's questions, sometimes in interdisciplinary groups.

The measures of success at Beloit College further blur traditional roles. Recast as researchers, students produce polished papers and also present their work to their research pod at the end of the summer and then to the college and community at a spring symposium. The program comes with an incentive to contribute to real-world research: acceptance at regional and national conferences and peer-reviewed publication comes with travel money and a bookstore credit. Measures of success recast faculty-student relationships as well. Faculty are paid to be faculty members in the eight-week program, and the program provides travel funding and stipends for collaborative research with students that leads to publication. In a flipping of roles, faculty success is encased in student success.

We see in Beloit College's comprehensive commitment to undergraduate research as well as in more limited course-based undergraduate research experiences the potential to recast undergraduate education as collaborative learning by breaking down the roles that students and faculty are expected to play. As an educational practice, undergraduate research is designed to value participation in shared problem-solving over other commitments that are wired into traditional faculty and student roles. By definition, undergraduate research makes students—people with identities and experiences—essential to the collaboration. Students are at the same time novices and de facto employees and researchers. Faculty step into the role of advisor and support staff and work on problems framed and solved in collaboration with others. Distributing responsibility for research comes with the requirement that experts trust and respect novices, and novices feel an obligation to be prepared to contribute what they can. There is now widespread agreement that such collaborations design space for critical questioning, reflecting on the experience, and grappling with uncertainty (Ryan and Deci 2000). The practice redefines student success as framing and solving real-world problems.

Undergraduate research is widely accepted as a high-impact practice across the curriculum. It is also a practice that is difficult to scale in large measure because it challenges the traditional division of labor in undergraduate education (Dolan 2017; Wolf 2018). The traditional curriculum is designed around the delivery of content by experts, not for collaborative learning. Incentives—whether grants and publications or completed courses and degrees—reward individuals. These challenges notwithstanding, the practice has the potential to change the roles that students, staff, and faculty are expected to play, shifting their attention to shared endeavors anchored in addressing real-world problems. These programs have the potential to pull faculty out of offices and labs and into networks that include and respect novices and disrupt existing research agendas based on input from diverse voices. They have the potential to push students to see undergraduate education as joining and contributing to communities of practice. And as we saw in the MSIs study, this practice can align student, staff, and faculty roles with the needs of a local community.

Conclusion: The Need for a Cognitive Shift

We are not alone in observing that the traditional division of labor is alive and well in American higher education. In her anthropology of college, Blum (2016) outlines the roles that students and faculty play. Students apply for admission and, on being admitted, complete discrete courses and earn grades by completing assigned activities. Those who complete the "right courses" with the "right grades" receive degrees. Getting it right means knowing and excelling at the role of student. Faculty are members of departments and disciplines first and foremost. Anchored in that identity, they individually and sometimes collectively design the courses that are formalized in syllabi. Faculty manage course activities, assess student participation, and assign grades. Some faculty advise students about course selection and college-going; a few supervise students in undergraduate research or community-based learning, though much of this work is taken on by an army of student services staff that does not figure much in Blum's anthropology. These invisible actors provide services, not instruction. Their roles are defined by programs: they recruit students and manage admission programs; advise students on course selection and provide tutoring; and often manage the co-curriculum. They do this all in support of students who learn from faculty.

We are not alone in seeking to blend traditional roles and responsibilities. In their often cited article on the future of undergraduate education, Barr and Tagg predicted in 1995 the blurring roles of learners and teachers, and the Boyer Commission report called for a "symbiotic relationship among all participants." Sadly, the traditional division of labor has proved to be very robust, surviving occasional attempts at disruption. Since 1995, classrooms have been "flipped" and designed around learning outcomes. Faculty have been invited to trade their role as "sage on the stage" for facilitator of learning, and students have been encouraged to be far more engaged in their learning. Advisors and financial aid staff have seized the initiative to foster student learning along with providing information and support. Learning management systems and social media—from Rate My Professor to Cluster Flunk—have altered the representation of who is doing what in undergraduate education. Moreover, some colleges and universities are providing "guided pathways" and exploring cross-functional teams of students, staff, and faculty (Bailey, Jaggars, and Jenkins 2015). These disruptions notwithstanding, everyday life on most campuses has not changed much.

Disrupting the traditional division of labor in higher education will require the kind of shift in cognitive frames that has swept across many professions (Argyris 1999; Edmondson 2012; Schön 1983). Rather than individual experts focused on their tasks, professionals increasingly find themselves in teams organized for shared problem-solving and increasingly in more loosely arranged collaborative units that form and reform as new problems come up (Engeström 2008). The received wisdom is that practitioners become more productive and persistent when they frame their shared endeavor as learning rather than performance, when they are oriented to attaining ideals and goals rather than preventing loss.

A reframing of roles is at the heart of this cognitive shift. Leaders become interdependent team members who rely on less experienced and less expert team members to guide their action; they learn with and from others in joint problem-solving. Team members expect to ask questions and find information about core tasks even though others may take the lead on completing those tasks. Indeed, all team members know that they were selected for the team because they bring perspectives, experiences, and knowledge that others—including those with greater expertise and others who have been working on the problem longer—do not have. Traditional hierarchical roles and responsibilities are transformed as teams are formed around solving shared problems that do not have "right answers" or all-encompassing solutions.

What does this mean for higher education? An institutional commitment to collaborative learning comes with an invitation to students, staff, faculty, and the communities served by higher education to take on new roles with blurry boundaries. All participants are asked to define their positions in the institution through working symbiotically with others rather than by drawing only on their personal traits or their cultural or economic capital or the positional roles that they inhabit. Every participant expects to be engaged in inquiry, and everyone is accountable to pushing shared problem-solving forward. Everyone expects to learn from, with, and for others. The MSIs embraced a new division of labor largely in part because the existing tradition in American higher education failed too many of the students that these institutions served and, in part, because faculty and students and staff came from more collectivist cultures. Blurring roles at most PWIs will be more challenging.

Is it worth the disruption? We believe it is. Blurring roles with respect to instruction, support, and research brings to the forefront an educational mission rooted in problem-solving and distributes the responsibility for achieving the mission. Distributing responsibility to educate all students across all participants, including students, creates more diverse points of connection to the educational mission for students, staff, and faculty. Enmeshed in a network rather than the traditional division of labor, they come to expect undergraduate education to take up real-world problems that are relevant to members of the campus community and, at the same time, to value and require the contributions of all participants in responding to these problems. Blending roles and responsibilities moves us toward the kind of undergraduate education that is needed.

CHAPTER 5

Receiving and Giving Feedback

As we began to envision undergraduate education as participation in collaborative networks, we became deeply interested in feedback. Networks run on feedback, and feedback practices are wired into undergraduate education. All institutions provide students with information—good, bad, or ugly—about what activities they are expected to take up and how they might engage those activities as well as information about the activities that they have completed. These feedback practices establish basic ground rules for learning and teaching at an institution, and they significantly influence how students approach their education. Beyond providing grades and ideas for improvement, feedback— both feed*forward* that guides students as they engage learning and teaching and feed*back* that provides them with information about their performances—tells students directly and indirectly what roles and identities are available to them, what sorts of relationships they can and will have with others, what learning matters, and what kinds of students and even what kinds of human beings they are becoming.

Too often in our colleges and universities, feedback practices reinforce the vision of undergraduate education as a solo journey to a degree. The feedback that matters is generated by teachers, and it spells out what the requirements are and how well students have satisfied those requirements. Framed this way, feedback leads students to view their education largely in terms of successes and failures, points and grades. In this chapter, we explore ways in which feedback practices might scaffold a different kind of education, one that invites students to expect to participate in ongoing back-and-forth dialogue with others and provides students with valuable information about how they are learning with, from, and for others.

The idea that feedback practices shape the educational experiences of students is hardly new. Decades of studies of feedback in higher education have shown that feedback can significantly enhance student learning (Shute 2008), increase the motivation of students (Cowan 2010), guide students along their educational journey, and provide students with assessments of their participation in networks of learners. Reviews of research on feedback (Evans 2013; Hattie and Timperley 2007; Shute 2008) agree on the basic contours of effective feedback: students receive responses to their work that encourage them to remain engaged in learning and assist them in making sense of past performances and improving future performances. Such feedback improves the capabilities of students to transfer their learning to new situations across the landscapes of their lives. When feedback is centered on student learning, arrives in time for use, and matches students' needs, it can promote student engagement and learning (Cowan 2010; Shute 2008) and often leads students to embrace participation in learning communities (Carless et al. 2011; Evans 2013). Calls for reform in undergraduate education have long included giving students much more formative feedback on their learning (Braxton, Eimers, and Bayer 1996; Myers and Myers 2015).

Not surprisingly, many colleges and universities publicly express an institution-wide commitment to providing students with feedback on their performance and, in some cases, formative feedback on what they could do to strengthen their work in the future—assessment for learning or learning-centered feedback (Bennett 2011; Cookson 2018; Evans 2013; Hawe and Dixon 2017; Stiggins 2002). That commitment notwithstanding, most of the feedback that students receive and give is about individual achievement, and not much is changing (Dawson et al. 2019; Orrell 2006; Shute 2008). Much of the feedback students receive is about past performances—grades and justifications for grades. Feedback on past performance rarely offers more than vague comments about the work that a student has done and what they need to do to improve their work. Moreover, feedback often fails to take into account how students approached their work or what their goals were (Boud and Molloy 2013). Feedback, even if well intended, is often viewed by students as control or criticism or false praise. One meta-analysis of research on feedback found that more than one-third of feedback interventions had negative effects on learning (Kluger and DeNisi 1996). Even when feedback stimulates engagement, it may provide little more than a "surface approach" to learning (McGarr and Clifford 2013). And far too often, the feedback provided offers relatively little guidance in preparing students to address the problems they are working on in the present or may work on in the future (Boud and Molloy 2013; Carless et al. 2011; Deeley and Bovill 2017; Perera et al. 2008; US Department of Education 2006).

Undergraduate students who are individual learners are especially prone to view feedback as a tactic for tallying gains. As they progress through undergraduate education, individual learners remain open to feedback about their learning to the extent that the information maps a clear way to accomplishment and certification (Dawson et al. 2019; Frost and Connolly 2015). Feedback from self, peers, and nonteachers is often suspect. While at times feedback on the learning of students seeks to position them as participants in dialogues about learning, most students remain individual learners whose driving purpose is to produce better performances. Feedback practices that promote collaborative learning—dialogue about shared endeavors and ways of interacting as well as reflecting on contrarian and marginalized perspectives and input—often remain on the margins because seeking out, offering, and using feedback that promotes collaborative learning risks deemphasizing the aspirations of individual learners.

In embracing institutional commitments to the success of all students, programs in the MSIs study routinely went beyond viewing feedback as certification of individuals' academic success. When we asked students at MSIs to identify practices that contributed to their success, they initially talked about grades. But when we probed, students often spoke of one-on-one conversations with faculty, staff, and their peers. During a focus group meeting, students in the nursing program at North Seattle Community College (NSCC) talked about giving one another feedback on how best to support not only the persistence but also the learning of one another. Students in this program also described inhabiting places—office hours, open labs, learning centers, study groups, Starbucks—where they encountered ongoing give-and-take as participants engaged in collaborative learning. These students attributed their success in the nursing program in large measure to their cultivating such habits as asking questions, sharing information, seeking help, experimenting, discussing mistakes, and seeking input from diverse voices.

With respect to giving and receiving feedback, three findings from across the 12 institutions in the MSIs study stand out. First, students told us that they saw feedback as an invitation to "ask their questions" and, as an NSCC student put it, "to build off what you now know rather than to find out that all of these chunks are missing." Second, engaging in feedback drew students into interdependent relationships with other students as well as staff and faculty. Students came to depend on others for feedforward to guide their performance before they tried it and then feedback to get details on what they actually did and how what they did compared with what they had hoped to do. Feedback helped them understand which of their behaviors were "okay" and also made them comfortable generating their own feedback about "how they are doing" and what needed to change if they were to do better. Third, most of the programs in the MSIs study created what an administrator at Chief Dull Knife College (CDKC) called "organically-forming cohorts" to amplify feedback. Staff and faculty at CDKC knew students well enough to bring them together in flexible partnerships formed around a shared problem. In these partnerships students worked together drawing on feedback on past performances and next steps, and, as a group, they unpacked feedback in dialogue with instructors. These informal cohorts served as echo chambers or what this administrator called "little band practice rooms." Together, students and teachers generated feedback, interpreted feedback, and put feedback to use. In the words of another CDKC administrator, these cohorts "exponentially increased the chances of somebody finding a way to work their way through wherever they're stuck on."

Participants in the CDKC program emphasized that embedding proactive feedback in organically forming cohorts to reframe and address a shared problem significantly enhanced students' learning. We came to appreciate how much a network of student learners can nourish collaborative learning through back-and-forth dialogues in which participants collectively engage in addressing the problem that they are pursuing and also the steps they are taking to solve it. Students across the institutions in the MSIs study described ways in which this networking enhanced their capacities to listen to the ideas of others, define and pursue problems and solutions collectively, and reflect on their own and others' contributions. Willing to embrace uncertainty and to engage in risk-taking in the pursuit of ideas, they described learning to view feedback as potentially valuable information to be interpreted with others and a pathway to deepen their relationships in ways that advanced their shared problem-solving.

Feedback practices that promote collaborative learning are learning-centered: they provide transparent information about the learning tasks that students take up as well as detailed information about the ways in which they have completed tasks and what they might do next in order to keep learning. The MSIs took up these practices largely to make undergraduate education more transparent for students who were entering an institution designed for other people's children. At PWIs learning-centered feedback practices not only make the curriculum more transparent, but they also have the potential to diversify ways of knowing and repositioning all students as problem-solvers. In this chapter, we explore three promising practices for facilitating the giving and receiving of feedback that promotes collaborative learning: establish multiple channels of feedback for everyone involved; establish spaces for participants to reflect on feedback; and share feedback on participation.

Establish Multiple Channels for Feedback from Diverse Participants

The idea that a learning-centered education depends on multiple channels of feedback on students' performances is not our idea. Again and again, studies describe learning-centered feedback in terms of a "landscape" (Evans 2013) or "partnership" (Deeley and Bovill 2017; Sommers 2006) or "dialogue" (Carless et al. 2011) that routinely provides honest, detailed, and potentially useful information to a network of learners and teachers along with opportunities to apply feedback in trying the same performance over again. As Haswell (2006) observed, feedback is a complex activity that makes use of all the communicative practices available in the context in which feedback is offered. When feedback is a respectful exchange of ideas about problem-solving in a network of "partners," the studies cited above agree that it not only spurs the development of individual learners but also transforms their experience from a solitary journey to participation in networks of learners.

Based on his review of decades of research, Evans (2013) portrays the emerging understanding of feedback as collaborative exchange. Rather than a singular intervention, what Evans calls "assessment feedback" circulates through sequences of collaborative exchange. Feedback is a representation of how individuals process information in a network focused on improving its capacity to solve the problems that the network is addressing—whether those problems are learning to write a paper in college or addressing pollution in a local stream. Along similar lines, we have come to think of feedback as a space of interaction and not simply discrete bits of information aimed at correcting behavior or understandings. The unit of analysis is, to use Evans's language, a "feedback landscape." A feedback landscape is shaped by how participants communicate, the roles and relationships of participants, and the tools that are available to them. A feedback landscape promotes interdependent relationships to the extent that participants parley with one another about what feedback will be circulated and how it will be circulated so that feedback becomes localized and intentional. In a feedback landscape that makes assessment feedback available, learners get the information they need while also accepting the obligation to seek out, question, and make use of that information. No less important, teachers are motivated to provide candid appraisals of performances that learners can use to better understand and enrich their participation in the collective endeavor.

Bottom line: the spaces in which feedback circulates shape what information circulates. Evans suggests that a feedback landscape in undergraduate education takes shape both within and across courses and disciplines, with each different network scaffolding engagement with a set of shared problems and communicating about their progress, challenges, and successes. Students and teachers move between these networks in taking up different problems. Each network provides guided practice in taking up problems and supporting dialogue that generates feedback on how students perceive and use feedback and in what ways their capacity to use feedback is changing.

Much of the recent research frames learning-centered feedback in higher education as both the participation in and the outcome of collaborative problem-solving. As they make and negotiate information about learning, participants map out the ways in which different kinds of feedback from different participants will be valued and used. They talk through how novices will take feedback from experts, how novices will give feedback to experts and other novices, and how different participants—students and instructors as well as external stakeholders—feel about giving and taking feedback. Teachers invest in how learners are learning and what uses they are making of different kinds of feedback. Students learn how to manage feedback on their development, including reflecting on their personal understanding of and reaction to feedback.

Experiments in cultivating learning-centered feedback landscapes abound. We now turn to three published studies of learning-centered feedback—Cary Moskovitz's Volunteer Expert Reader approach, Daniel Reinholz's Peer-Assisted Reflection, and Nancy Sommers's reflections on the Harvard Writing Project—that flesh out ways in which learning-centered feedback landscapes position learners and teachers in relationship to one another.

Volunteer Expert Reader Approach

In a project funded by the National Science Foundation, Cary Moskovitz (2017) implemented the Volunteer Expert Reader (VER) approach to provide engineering students with learning-centered feedback on their writing from volunteer alumni engineers—readers who have direct experiences with the rhetorical contexts in which engineers write—as well as teachers and peers. VER was implemented at Duke University in an entry-level mechanical engineering course titled Engineering Innovations in which students take on real-world design challenges in groups. While enriching channels of feedback is central to his model, Moskovitz's conceptualization of feedback is no less important. He defines feedback as an invitation to "reflection, rethinking and revision" about a "meaningful communication task" (2). Detailed class assignments and volunteer training materials focus participants' attention on this shared endeavor. Meanwhile, dialogue is facilitated by a "project manager" who starts the process by introducing participants to one another, making participant commitments explicit, and then issuing regular reminders about their timeline. Readers are trained in providing "reader-based feedback." Students provide drafts and responses to feedback.

Students in VER receive multiple sources of feedback from reviewers with diverse perspectives and experiences, such as working engineers, coauthors, and instructors. Feedback—intentionally separated from grading or correcting writing—focuses on readers' responses to the effectiveness of the design report at the center of the course. Transmitted through email, written comments, and conversations, feedback includes divergent and even contradictory responses to elements of the design report that students interpret based on the interests and experiences of each of their readers. Rather than waiting for grades, students engage in cycles of interaction with their expert reader while other channels of feedback remain open. Assessment of this project found that students wanted more feedback earlier in their design process and that they were interested in more real-time, face-to-face discussions of their work. Many students hoped for more feedback from engineers in the field that could help them solve problems like engineers in their future courses as well as in the workplace.

Peer-Assisted Reflection

In a project that grew out of an Institute of Educational Sciences predoctoral training grant, Daniel Reinholz elaborated on a model of "peer-assisted reflection" (PAR) that separates feedback from grades and positions students and teachers to look at problems in mathematics classes as sources of creativity and innovation. Each week students in a course who are participating in PAR draft a solution to at least one "PAR problem." These problems "(1) are easy to start but hard to master, (2) have multiple solution paths, and (3) are more than just computations" (Reinholz 2018, 654). The feedback process begins with students coming together during class time to review and discuss solutions to a sample problem and then drafting their individual solution to the PAR problem, reviewing their own work, and selecting aspects of their draft solution on which they need feedback. Once all students have submitted their work and their reflections on their work, they review sample problems and solutions as well as a peer's solutions and reflections and, in turn, offer feedback that they shared in class discussions and peer conferences. Feedback in hand, students revise their solution of the PAR problem and then resubmit it.

Each PAR cycle is framed in terms of the work of science: scientists seek out peer reviewers to advance their work. Coming up with more complete answers to problems is almost a side effect. Becoming able to provide meaningful feedback to a peer is the driving purpose of the assignment. Students review not only model solutions to problems but also models of feedback on draft solutions. Through engaging in back-and-forth communication about the quality of potential solutions, students learn as much about the process of solving a problem as about the correctness of a solution.

The Harvard Study of Undergraduate Writing

Reflecting on the findings from a study of 400 Harvard students during their four years of college, Nancy Sommers (2006) came to understand effective feedback as a "partnership" that mixes honest critique with instruction. In this partnership, teachers engage students as apprentice scholars, and students remain open to ideas to take with them to their next assignment and to being engaged in solving "big problems" and not simply learn what is correct. In the Harvard study, feedback that contributes to students' growth as writers is viewed as an opportunity to engage in "back-and-forth exchange between student and teacher, writer and reader" (251). Through these exchanges with different teachers, the expectations that a student writer is meeting become explicit iteratively, one step at a time, and the writer is open to deciding how to meet those expectations as a whole person. As emphasized by Sommers (2006), these partnerships are about more than individual accomplishment: "As our students teach us, their papers don't end when they turn them in for a grade, nor do our comments end when we write them. The partnership between writer and reader, between student and teacher, creates something new—a collection of ideas that are larger than the paper itself, ideas milling around, moving forth into the world, across the drafts." (255–56)

Across these three projects, feedback fuels critical dialogue in solving real-world problems among diverse participants who expect to gather information developed in their shared problem-solving. The focus on feedback in each project brings participants together to address complex problems. Students have the opportunity to take up problems that are not simple computations completed to show a teacher what they know. Instead, students and teachers work together on problems in a community of problem-solvers—engineers, scientists, researchers, writers. The feedback conversation moves beyond completing class assignments for points to addressing wicked problems that do not have single correct answers or a single approach and that have meaning outside a single course or educational program. This is the case even in a college algebra class where the problem is not simply solving an equation but becoming a scientist who can explain to other scientists the way an approach to that problem moves toward a solution.

By engaging teachers and students as co-learners who are jointly engaging in complex problem-solving, the underlying purpose of feedback is taking up what learners do and how their participation does and does not move their problem-solving toward a possible solution. Explanations of how attempts at addressing problems move toward and away from solutions bring learners and teachers together in problem-solving partnerships. Novices' attempts at solutions are as important to the process as experts' understandings of how such problems have been solved. Feedback is a dialogue about progress the network is making on solutions to shared problems rather than on the "correctness" of an individual's behavior or contribution.

Engaged with shared problems that cannot be defined or solved in a single "correct" way, the learners and teachers in these studies engage in critical dialogue about activity—both past performances and upcoming attempts—rather than assertions about the capabilities of individuals or the correctness of products. Each project underscores the need for honest and detailed information about past performances and about ways in which learners might approach similar performances in the future. At the same time, detailed instructive feedback does not foreclose the process of problem-solving. Teachers cannot say what any particular learner needs to do. They can explain how they perceive a performance, what that performance produced, and how that performance compares with other performances. Without exceptions, their offerings are about a process aimed at solving problems that can be solved in more than one way. Their goal is not to control a learner's behavior but to generate information about how an approach to a shared problem has moved closer to solving that problem even if that approach appears to be a dead end.

Because each feedback dialogue recognizes students' attempts as valid and remains open to innovation in problem-solving, students and teachers embrace uncertainty and contradiction rather than looking for confirmation and consensus. In the VER approach, engineering students hear from peers, faculty, Teaching Assistants, and working engineers—"readers" who have been trained to offer "reader-based feedback" on an explicit design challenge. Readers are expected to share with learners their "reactions to the drafts considering the intention of the writing and the context for which it was written." Rather than having readers "correct student work, [reader-based feedback] guidelines encourage readers to describe and explain the aspects of the draft they find effective and those they find to be ineffective, inappropriate to the context, or otherwise problematic—through the lens of the experienced engineer" (Moskovitz 2017, 9).

In each of these feedback landscapes, each participant responds based on prior experiences in solving the kinds of problems with which the network is engaged. In both the VER and PAR approaches as well as in the Harvard study feedback partnerships, performance expectations are explicit and guide students and reviewers: reviewers respond to the same performance from their "lens." Respect for the intentions of students and reviewers is written into the process. Throughout this process, reviewers with a variety of experiences often respond differently, and this variation in responses calls attention to varying aspects of a performance and often produces different, sometimes contradictory, assessments and recommendations. The feedback process requires learners to make sense of conflicting responses to their work. This approach makes managing uncertainty about how to use feedback to move forward on solving the problem at hand part of the collaborative process.

Through critical dialogues focused on solving shared problems, making and using feedback becomes an integral part of the process of problem-solving. Developing the capacity to use feedback is not extra work taken up by students who are not college ready. It is a program requirement. In the VER approach, engineering students discuss revisions with readers; in a PAR cycle, beginning math students speculate about possible approaches to sample problems and discuss the approaches they have chosen with peers and an instructor. College writers at Harvard emphasize that what makes feedback transformative are conversations about specific ideas with an engaged reader who expects them to rewrite. In each project, successful learners learn how to give and use feedback.

Across these projects, formative feedback asks learners and teachers to value looking back at specific performances—solving an algebra problem, writing a report, writing in a college class—and reflecting on how their performances were produced and how to make use of feedback to approach the same and related performances differently. Feedback circulates through a "call and response": students take the lead with ideas, and faculty listen to and extend those ideas rather than taking them over or displacing them (Sommers 2006, 252). This communication process validates students as full participants in real-world problem-solving. Participation comes with an expectation to respect and to be accountable to other participants. Getting a problem "right" means making use of feedback and having improved as a participant in a network engaged in problem-solving. Using feedback means viewing a reviewer's response not as a judgment of personal ability but as an opportunity to contribute to a network. Feedback is taken seriously by all participants.

These three projects are nested in a growing body of research that points to ways in which a feedback landscape can promote student development. We see in this work a path to transforming the basic structure of undergraduate education. Examples scattered across the landscape of higher education suggest that the cultivation of a learning-centered pattern of feedback can change an institution and alter the spaces in which students learn. For more than a decade, a growing number of faculty in higher education have blended digital tools into traditional courses so that students work out problems in the open, receive feedback on their approach from multiple participants in the course through multiple modes, and then work out the problems again (Sun et al. 2018). Along the way, students have come to expect timely input on their emerging practice to be available digitally. The University of Arizona is one of many institutions that have begun redesigning classrooms to allow students to approach problems with and for others, scribbling on tabletop whiteboards and tablets or working together at a computer monitor. In the University of Arizona Collaborative Learning Spaces, students work on a class problem that takes center stage, and this space is designed to document approaches to solving problems, annotating these approaches, and trying the problems again.

Beyond improving student learning, a learning-centered feedback landscape invites all participants—students as well as teachers—to see education as engaging in shared problem-solving that obligates everyone to generate, discuss, and use feedback on problem-solving and, in so doing, embrace the uncertainty that comes with incorporating multiple channels of information as part of finding the way to solutions. This feedback landscape can put collaborative learning at the center of undergraduate education. In the remainder of this chapter we explore two design features that help make this happen: space for reflection and transparency about participation.

Create Spaces for Participants to Reflect on Feedback

When viewed as spaces for collaboration rather than the transmission of information, feedback practices invite learners to see themselves as collaborative learners who are potentially valuable sources of information. Collaborative learning depends on participants taking time throughout their problem-solving to reflect on and represent their respective contributions to addressing shared problems along with their understanding of the ways in which their community-of-practice is engaged in and making progress toward solutions and identifying future challenges that it might pursue. Collaborative learners are willing to step back from doing the work of problem-solving to document and question the process so as to clarify their burning questions and curate a rich pool of resources by learning from and with others and representing what they have learned in their shared problem-solving.

As we asked students, staff, and faculty in the MSIs study about what contributed to students' learning, the importance of informal spaces for reflection kept coming up. Students and faculty members observed, often in passing, that required written reflections on the process of problem-solving were often as likely in mathematics classes as in English classes. We observed STEM faculty at North Seattle Community College (NSCC) teaching students how to review slides and textbooks ahead of class and asking them to visually represent their understanding of course content during class. Two of the institutions in the MSIs study were experimenting with math emporiums, and at the center of these programs was the expectation that students would break away from traditional class discussions and work with their peers or teacher-coaches to reflect on where they might not be understanding course content or the challenges of becoming a mathematics problem-solver.

One NSCC faculty member named the process of stepping away from problem-solving as "looping": students stepped away from course work to get "a small piece down" and "connect" it to the problems that they were learning to solve in the class and the understanding of biological systems they would need as nurses. Then they stepped back to share the connections they had made. "Back, forth, back, forth, loop, loop, loop, loop." During class, this faculty member asked students how they knew what they knew, often putting students in groups to share their reflections on how they learned a concept. She expected them to represent their current understanding symbolically, in writing, and often with images. She also gave them time to return to and annotate their representations of course content.

As we listened to students, staff, and faculty describe their approaches to reflection, we came to appreciate that for them reflection was not only a practice but also an educational outcome. They were engaged in what the authors of *How People Learn* (2000) described as a metacognitive approach to education: students were learning strategies for "explicating, elaborating, and monitoring the understanding necessary for independent learning" (67). They were practicing with models that guided reflection and participating in a setting in which understanding is jointly negotiated. By looping, students stepped back from their problem-solving to generate their own feedback on how they were approaching problems, why they were taking those approaches, and what results they were achieving. As importantly, students expected to share with others new understandings of course content, new solutions to problems, and new processes for solving problems. Teachers established spaces in which sharing was routine.

This kind of reflection was not simply self-evaluation. Students are often not particularly good at evaluating their own learning and generating the feedback that they need to move forward (Evans 2013). Looping involves students learning how to describe and analyze their own learning practices in light of feedback they receive from peers and experts. The instructors at the MSIs were scrambling to find ways to teach this kind of reflection and to practice it with their students. One SDCC math faculty mused that he was infusing reflection on problem-solving into an already packed curriculum. He did so because he saw students' progress when they became able to talk about what they were doing and why. Their success, he strongly believed, was worth transforming his classes. Decades of research on learning confirm his belief.

Infusing reflection into the curriculum seems to have great potential to transform not just courses but the undergraduate experience as well. The Teaching for Transfer (TFT) course developed by Kathleen Blake Yancey and others at Florida State University over the past decade serves as a case study. The TFT curriculum emerged from inquiry into a first-year composition curriculum "*designed* to support students' transfer of writing knowledge and practice" to other settings (Yancey, Robertson, and Taczak 2014, 4). Put simply, the curriculum is designed to develop students' capacities to solve challenges in writing across and beyond their education. The curriculum has three core curricular elements: "(1) key rhetorical terms, (2) reflection, and (3) students' articulation of a theory of writing" (Taczak and Robertson 2016, 45). In a TFT course, reflection is both a key word and a practice. In class, students read and discuss what reflection is and how it relates to writing. Most assignments ask students to reflect on how they are making use of course concepts to do the work of writing. In-class and out-of-class activities ask students to engage routinely in a four-part practice: "(1) look backward to recall previous knowledge, which could include prior writing experiences, different reading assignments, and past knowledge about writing; (2) look inward to review the current writing situation they are working in; (3) look forward to project how their current knowledge about writing connects to other possible academic writing situations; and (4) look outward to theorize how the role of their current identities as reflective writing practitioners connects to larger academic writing situations."(46).

Findings from assessment of the project show that students in a TFT course take the time to explain how what they have done might inform what they might do in other settings. They practice determining what knowledge and practices to roll forward. Perhaps most important, they "theorize" ways in which they can contribute to real-world situations and not merely fulfill course assignments to receive grades. They are invited to envision their education as preparation for communicating ideas in other classes and in the professions to which they aspire.

The TFT project is focused primarily on promoting the capacity of individual students to transfer their writing knowledge and practices. We suggest that this framework also formalizes looping and describes a feedback landscape that supports collaborative learning. Making space for reflection requires making reflection a routine activity in shared endeavors. Learners are invited to probe a real problem space and try solving real problems together. Addressing a problem triggers reflection—this is part of the script. As they reflect, students *look back* and, with input from others, validate their attempt: they did indeed try the problem and brought to that prior experiences, knowledge, and skills. Looking back means *looking inward* and engaging in self-assessment about their initial foray, and how it did or did not move toward their intended outcomes. Reflection does not stop with self-assessment. Learners also *look forward and outward*, projecting ways in which their knowledge and skills as well as their identities as problem solvers position them to contribute in their subsequent engagement in networks of problem-solvers.

By including space for reflection, a feedback landscape guides learners to probe the designated problem space with self-assessment in mind. Far from simple evaluation of a performance using abstract criteria, each participant reflects on how they might contribute to the shared endeavor. Reflection requires individuals to negotiate between multiple channels of feedback as they make sense of their own contributions and their next steps. Spaces for reflection are spaces in which learners expect to listen to others and to deal with uncertainty and often conflicting information as they crystallize and express what they are bringing to the shared endeavor. Feedback that makes space for reflection sets learners up to return to problem-solving informed by feedback from themselves and others.

An undergraduate education that takes reflection seriously creates space through assignments, activities, and assessments that invite students, staff, and faculty to look back at and claim learning that they have done so as to bring knowledge, experience, and skill to what they are doing now and imagine doing next. Writing reflectively, Yancey reminds us, is a *mechanism for claiming and legitimating learning*" (2016, 305; emphasis in original). Designing reflection into undergraduate education means that participants routinely unsettle what they thought they knew, seek out feedback from others, and offer feedback to others.

Share Feedback on Stakeholder Participation

Along with providing space for reflection, a feedback landscape that promotes collaborative learning routinely publishes information about the progress that participants are making in their shared problem-solving. The programs in the MSIs study shared several kinds of feedback. To begin, students we spoke with often mentioned that they needed feedback on their progress—often grades—immediately and frequently, and faculty conceded that keeping gradebooks in learning management systems up-to-date was critical in a learning-centered feedback landscape. CDKC and EPCC used computerized dashboards to help remedial English and math students track their progress in real time. Faculty at these two MSIs reviewed dashboards before class to decide what to cover and how to form groups. At SDCC and La Sierra, mentors tracked and responded to students' completion of benchmarks in a timely manner.

But it's not all about grades and milestones. The MSIs were peppered with informal opportunities for students to observe and learn from the experiences and strategies of others. Students described watching one another in classes, looking for behaviors and strategies that they might adopt and adapt. They emphasized that part of the value of Supplemental Instruction and peer mentoring programs was the chance to interact with someone who had recently completed a course they were taking. The experiences of these near peers were often sources of inspiration and motivation; their knowledge of short cuts and lore was often invaluable. Faculty designed group exercises not only so students could work together to solve problems and produce artifacts but also so that they could watch one another contribute to the processes through which they arrived at solutions. Students frequently worked out solutions together, collaborating throughout the problem-solving process.

Students, staff, and faculty in MSIs also shared their fears and dreams. Students of color and students who were learning English told us about finding hope in conversations about their feeling like an imposter or negotiating racism or balancing two cultures. EPCC staff who were immigrants shared what it was like for them to pursue a college education in English. Native American faculty and staff at Tribal Colleges and African American scientists at HBCUs told us about talking with minoritized students about what it meant to get an education in the face of overt racism.

The Peer-Led Team Learning (PLTL) program at Morehouse College represents the kind of open sharing of feedback that we encountered across the programs in the MSIs study (Gasman et al. 2017). PLTL, an innovative approach that has been shown to promote the retention and success of students in STEM classes, is much more than peer-assessment or peer review. Actively involved in PLTL, faculty members develop and provide learning content "modules" for PLTL workshops that are tethered to course content. These workshops are facilitated by peers who have completed the course and have been trained to facilitate collaborative learning. As we listened to students and staff talk about this approach at Morehouse, it was clear that they were redefining conventional feedback that students receive in STEM courses. Students at Morehouse described PLTL as a network of black men in which "achievement" did not simply mean individual ability to master content. They defined achievement as engaged participation in which students shared their understanding of ideas and solutions to problems and then provided one another with feedback on their participation and contributions. Students talked about viewing the difficult gateway courses they were completing not merely as content to be acquired but as opportunities to make of use of content as novice scientists and, more importantly, as members of a network of Black men who were making it through a rigorous science education. Again and again, they described how they were trying out, developing, and practicing with tools with others—from brainstorming with others to implementing trusted ways to solve a problem to talking, drawing, or writing through a simulation of a solution.

In the PLTL network at Morehouse College, what individuals were doing as well as what results their participation netted and even what grades they were getting was all out in the open. PLTL groups were able to generate rich feedforward: participants described approaches they planned to take, and both peers and leaders—students who had already completed the course—asked questions about those approaches. Leaders were trained not to control interactions and get students to solutions but instead to discuss problem-solving approaches and engage the group in elaborating, evaluating, and refining their approaches. Conversations continued until each member contributed what they could and found what they needed. Leaders had access to information about members' course performance, and members described feeling an obligation to share how they were doing with their "brothers." They shared a commitment to strengthening the capabilities of all members to solve problems; rather than judging one another's performances as successes and failures, those performances—and feedback on those performances—were mined to better understand how to approach problems. Part of that process was regular "check-ins" on the emotional status of members. Members who felt frustrated, overwhelmed, or inadequate often found that others also felt that way and explored paths to "state[s] of mind" that might better serve them.

The open sharing of stakeholder participation in the Morehouse PLTL program and other programs in the MSIs study represent, we believe, a path to a nontraditional undergraduate education—an education in which students and faculty expect to work together on solving real-world problems as a community and can talk about performance without fear. In institutions that serve diverse students, this kind of open sharing of feedback depends on and can promote what Asao Inoue (2015) has called an "antiracist assessment ecology." Inoue describes a feedback landscape in which learners and teachers share responsibility and negotiate what work each will do. The focus of the landscape is on "labor"—the effort and time that participants put in—rather than products to be evaluated. In Inoue's first-year composition curriculum, the time that each assigned reading will take is estimated, and acts of reading are made visible in postings and reflections. Writing is work that happens in iterative phases, from invention to revision exercises and back again, that make the process visible. Reflection is continuous representation of productive thinking—and responding to other's productive thinking—about the work of reading and writing. Assessing writing means articulating "descriptive judgments" based on co-constructed rubrics. Class projects emerge from the work of reading, reflection, writing, and assessing, and each of these core activities is negotiated by the class. Working together, the class designs a project rubric that makes explicit the qualities of proficient projects and a writer's rubric that articulates each writer's expected labor. The class also revises and agrees to a grading contract that details what amount of labor leads to what grade. Since standards and expectations are developed with and for students, students are better able to shift their energy from figuring out how to earn grades to doing the work of writing.

In an antiracist assessment ecology, feedback does not judge the quality of student writers or their work against abstract criteria. Instead, feedback describes what diverse readers—students and teachers—see in student work based on commitments that all share, commitments that are published so that students can draw on them in workshops and writing conferences. Students are involved in critically describing expectations, explaining the ways in which they do and do not see those expectations in their own and the work of others, and describing the kind of labor involved in producing work that meets expectations. Since students share feedback, they often have to negotiate conflicting assessments and reflect on how to make descriptive judgments and how to use descriptive judgements. In this kind of feedback landscape, feedback becomes information to support each student's learning in a context in which performance standards are already raced, classed, and gendered. Because what learning and standards involved are out in the open, students and teachers stop "correcting" learners and become engaged with supporting learners as they make sense of their own learning and decide how to manage institutional standards. Students and teachers come to expect conflicting feedback and uncertainty as they move forward. They question, reflect on, and own their contributions and, as importantly, value the contributions of others.

We believe that feedback landscapes in which participants negotiate expectations about performance pave the way for an education that is responsive to diverse learners, positioning all learners as full participants rather than judging some as unready or unprepared. In this kind of feedback landscape, the participation of individuals is out in the open and becomes part of a shared endeavor. Feedback ceases to be judgmental and becomes what James Paul Gee (2003) and others call a "learning reward cycle." Information about their current performance begins to entice learners to try and try again even after not realizing their own expectations on a previous attempt or feeling like the endeavor itself is uninteresting. Making and using information about their performance, whatever else the learner produces, constitutes meaningful learning because making and using information about current performance is, in part, what the network is about. In collaborative learning, problems are solved through the efforts of all. Feedback becomes a way of documenting those efforts, keeping track of what is working and what is not, and always looking for ideas that move the network toward solutions.

Conclusion: From Grades to Information about Participation

For more than half a century, there has been a call for feedback aimed at advancing the learning of students in our nation's colleges and universities. The emphasis on final examinations has shifted to some extent to a focus on continuing assessment in which students are given more feedback that is learning-centered. The underlying intent of many of these calls is to engage students in feedback "dialogues," "partnerships," or "landscapes" in which the focus is on becoming someone who solves problems rather than on the "correctness" of a performance that the student has already completed. In a feedback network, the person providing feedback—a peer, a teacher, students themselves—elaborates the problem space, calling attention to specific knowledge and skills that are relevant and to next steps to be taken. Feedback is iterative and invites students to return the same performance multiple times to work on specific goals. When that feedback is aimed at building capacity rather than certifying learning, feedback can make a very meaningful contribution to student learning (Evans 2013; Shute 2008).

We believe that along with improving student outcomes, a learning-centered feedback landscape can help an institution sustain a commitment to collaborative learning. Information about expectations and activities can position individuals to expect to develop more promising ideas for engaging shared problems through dialogue that obligates everyone to generate, discuss, and use feedback in their problem-solving. In a learning-centered feedback landscape, it is safe for novices to be uncertain and to make partial attempts at solving problems with others, for feedback practices outline expectations about contributing and guide second and third attempts. Institutions that make a commitment to collaborative learning sustain that commitment in part through establishing and nurturing a learning-centered feedback landscape.

Learning-centered feedback is indispensable in developing and sustaining a widely shared commitment to collaborative problem-solving. Feedback enables participants in a network to reflect on how they might proceed, what they and others are contributing, and how others are responding to their contributions. When feedback is wired into and fuels a learning community, an institution has incorporated collaboration into its mission, built shared ways of expressing a commitment to collaboration, and rescripted roles and practices such that everyone is expected to learn from, with, and for others. This commitment is sustained as the institution redesigns organizational structures to support spaces for networks of students and teachers to routinely communicate about progress on the inquiry that brings them together. In short, feedback has the potential to distribute problem-solving in networks of students and teachers along with rewarding reflection, unlearning, and second tries at problem-solving.

CHAPTER 6

Anchoring the Curriculum in Shared Problem-Solving

This entire book has been driven by the assumption that problem-solving is a bedrock "twenty-first century skill" and that, as the National Research Council suggested in *Education for Life and Work,* our colleges and universities should be educating problem-solvers. Schooling needs to incorporate reading, writing, and arithmetic, but what is demanded of it now is the education of people who can apply what they have learned in new situations and who know "how, why, and when to apply this knowledge to answer questions and solve problems" (2012, 6).

From our perspective, shared problem-solving is the driver of collaborative learning. Collaborative learners come together in networks that value the perspectives and ideas of others in conducting inquiry aimed at cultivating promising ideas to address shared problems. To engage in collaborative learning is to be an active participant in shared problem-solving who embraces the obligation to contribute to and add value to the network, question themselves and others, contemplate, and share their insights while engaged in joint problem-solving. In this chapter, we propose anchoring the curriculum in first-hand experiences in solving real–world problems that face actual communities. Rather than a means to amass a set of experiences and credentials that accrue to the benefit of an individual, an education anchored in problem-solving places major emphasis on time spent engaging directly in solving problems shared by others with others. Student success in college is measured in terms of progress in students' becoming skilled problem-solvers and solving local problems.

We begin the chapter by proposing that an undergraduate education for the twenty-first century should be anchored in shared problem-solving that is focused on solving local problems and, in turn, we explore how to begin building a curriculum around local issues. In the following sections of the chapter, we explore two features of a curriculum anchored in shared problem solving: formal and informal opportunities for community-engaged learning and opportunities for students, staff, and faculty to practice entrepreneurship. We conclude by suggesting that the curricular opportunities for collaborative learning discussed in this chapter provide a foundation for a culturally sustaining undergraduate education that recognizes the problems that motivate the diverse students now attending college, draws on the resources that they bring to college, and boosts their engagement in their own education (Ladson-Billings, 2014). Throughout the chapter we draw on initiatives from colleges and universities across the nation to suggest how institutions can develop a curriculum that is anchored in shared problem-solving.

Reframing Problem-Solving as Solving Local Problems

Problem-solving, critical thinking, and adaptive learning have long topped lists of the knowledge and skills that undergraduates need to acquire (Bransford, Brown, and Cocking 2000; Commission on the Future of Undergraduate Education 2017; Fitzpatrick 2007; National Research Council 2012). Many policymakers and educators emphasize that students must engage in a "deeper" kind of learning: problem-solving that transfers not just from course to course and level to level but from school to the outside world. Building upon John Dewey's call more than a century ago to link learning in school to learning in everyday life, contemporary discussions of undergraduate education in this country often include arguments for more emphasis engaging students in analysis of relevant content, real-world problems, and research (Bain 2004; Bean 2011).

Strategies for placing real-world problem-solving as a cornerstone of undergraduate education have been elaborated on since William Kilpatrick promoted "project learning" in 1918 (for reviews, see Condliffe and Associates 2017; Thomas 2000). Largely encompassing project-based learning and problem-based learning (PBL), this educational strategy encourages teachers to provide students with opportunities to take on "complex tasks, based on challenging questions or problems, that involve students in design, problem-solving, decision making, or investigative activities; give students the opportunity to work relatively autonomously over extended periods of time; and culminate in realistic products or presentations" (Thomas 2000, 1). The goal of project learning is to engage students in their own education (Moursund 1999), often through collaborative projects in which they take on "driving questions" in communities of inquiry (Krajcik et al. 1994; Marx et al. 1997) and share the results of their problem-solving with public audiences outside of school.

Project learning has proven to be a beneficial strategy for cultivating individual problem-solvers, and albeit less frequently, project learning serves as a pathway to collaborative learning. Most project learning assignments include instruction on how to contribute to a team, assessments of team dynamics, and individual reflection on how each member's participation on the team affected that member's learning (Oliveri, Lawless, and Molloy 2017). Yet, in most project-based and problem-based learning in our colleges and universities, learning with, from, and for communities impacted by real-world problems remains a secondary goal. PBL—including group problem-solving—is usually designed to engage individual learners more deeply in their own education.

Our conversations with students, staff, and faculty at the MSIs pointed us to an alternative way of thinking about projects and framing problem-solving: engaging in collaborative inquiry aimed at solving local problems. This framing for project learning emerged in many programs as a way to make school relevant. In reflecting on the difficulties that most students were facing in solving problems in physics, a faculty member in the sciences at Chief Dull Knife College told us that most of his students begin STEM programs without understanding why they are learning math and science. In conversations about math and science courses, his students portrayed their role as coming up with the "right answers" to problems posed by instructors. They assumed that the content in STEM courses was owned by instructors and that they needed to focus on passing classes. Few of his students knew an engineer or scientist who worked on the Reservation. When these students tried to address the problems they were assigned as homework in math and science classes, they struggled to come up with solutions. When similar problems showed up on tests, they often froze. Students frequently described feeling frustrated that the problems they were expected to solve were disconnected from their lives, and often they "disengaged" and then disappeared from college.

To address this challenge, STEM faculty at CDKC began talking with students in required STEM courses about relationships between what they were learning in class and what can be done with that learning outside of class. Developing what this science instructor called a practical "framework to hang ideas on" helped students find their purpose in college and move successfully through STEM programs. Faculty at CDKC—especially mathematics faculty—began to use class time to build conceptual frameworks "from scratch" with students. Faculty and students also discussed "what we use that for."

A mathematics faculty member at CDKC asked students about the games that they played outside of college so that he could connect mathematical concepts to frameworks that students already used when they thought abstractly and made generalizations. This faculty member emphasized that his primary goal was not getting students through a class. "What matters," he emphasized, "is what they learn and that it makes a difference and is going to continue to make a difference for the rest of their lives." Instead of having students using formulas to solve problems put to them by the instructor, one of his colleagues developed "inquiry problems" that invited remedial math students to use concepts they were learning to "do something I might need to do someday." Other faculty engaged STEM students who were still working their way through college algebra on grant-funded research projects. STEM faculty at CDKC emphasized again and again the importance of identifying problems that students found, as one math faculty put it, to be "practical and applicable to me."

A CDKC student explained to us that what made school problems "practical and applicable" was that students were given opportunities to participate in their "worlds," whether that meant the problems were related to getting a good job or sustaining a family or, for her, learning Cheyenne. When we asked this student what role CDKC played in preparing her to transfer to a PWI, she didn't hesitate: "I got my internship job that really brought a lot. It took me places." When asked to elaborate on why the internship mattered, she said that it was using the math and science she was learning on an NSF-funded project to develop a water filter for application in the developing world. As she worked alongside students and staff from the University of Montana, she came to "love" STEM. Her education provided opportunities to "explore the world" and "make something of yourself."

Placing "practical and applicable problems" at the center of undergraduate education clearly had a major impact on how students at the MSIs navigated through their undergraduate experience. Students consistently linked "our college" and their education to collaborating with others in addressing such problems as water quality, health challenges in a family or a community, preservation of a language, the development of local businesses, and success in college. They sought an education that makes for a better life for families and communities. In response, the programs in the MSI study created opportunities for students to take up shared real-world problems with others who were already at work on those problems.

The programs in the MSI study welcome newcomers into networks that are working on solving problems relevant to students' communities. Faculty were not shy about putting first-year undergraduates to work on complex and ill-formed problems that are difficult to frame and rarely have a single solution. All of the MSI programs engaged students with the problem of making undergraduate education accessible for students not well served by traditional American higher education. And most of the programs invited students to become engaged in addressing challenges faced by the communities from which they came. Students contributed to programs that helped get students of color—often including themselves—through college and into the professions, provide healthcare to communities poorly served, deal with local environmental issues, strengthen governance in local communities, start local businesses, confront racism, and sustain nondominant cultural traditions. Student after student at the MSIs told us that their education was not only about "getting ahead" but also about using their education to address problems and capitalize on opportunities in their communities.

Listening to students' understanding of the purpose of a college education pushed us to rethink the role of problem-solving in undergraduate education. We have come to view problem-solving in higher education as something that people do rather than as a teaching strategy. Students, faculty, and staff are continually engaged in solving problems, from figuring out how to ask a question in class to identifying sources of water contamination in a local watershed to completing a degree that provides entry into a social group or a profession. Practical and applicable problems are not so much tasks given by teachers as needs that emerge in the situations in which people find themselves.

Rather than the choices of a decision maker or an algorithm that yields a correct answer to a question, we have come to view problem-solving as participation in social practices that shape the problems that individuals and groups choose to address and how they pursue them. Sometimes the problem and process is immediate: the uncertainty of first-year students is resolved through regular meetings with more experienced near-peers.

More often, we observed students and teachers taking up real-world problems through problem-solving processes that were iterative and emergent. The problem of passing a course in fluid dynamics is distantly related to satisfying a desire to belong to a community of engineers, get a job as an engineer, or become prepared to design and maintain roads in a local community. The nature of the problem and the most meaningful solutions usually develop over time.

We have settled on a designer's approach to problem-solving. Designers rarely accept problems at face value; instead, "they start by trying to understand what the real issues are" (Norman 2013, 218). In solving problems, designers talk to people affected by the problem. They listen to how others frame issues, consider diverse causes and solutions, and question the ways in which problems have previously been framed and solved. While designers often make use of past solutions and first principles, they define and explore problems and solutions abductively from the ground up, sketching prototypes, and then refining solutions in a dialogue with those affected by the problem (Cross 2011).

This view of problem-solving changes the role of problems in undergraduate education. Because they are engaged with problems faced by the communities of the students they serve, the MSIs had already embraced this view of problem-solving. Institutions invested in a traditional undergraduate education may find this approach disruptive in large part because it requires them to redefine who students are as problem-solvers. A designer's view of undergraduate education positions students from the time they begin their education as people who are aware of many of the problems that their communities are facing and who often bring an interest in solving some of these problems. If their education is to enhance their capabilities as problem-solvers, that education will include opportunities to explore real-world problems in which they have a stake and work iteratively on solutions. The curriculum becomes a sandbox full of tools—from technologies and ways of interacting to rules, relationships, and distributions of labor. In that sandbox, undergraduates can benefit from observing others using tools to solve problems and also try out tools that they think are likely to be useful in the future. They have plentiful opportunities to sketch out partial solutions and build prototypes, get feedback, and make improvements—all the while meeting "real needs." They have chances to become Paul Hanstedt's "wicked graduates."

Unfortunately, relatively few undergraduate students in American higher education have opportunities to become this kind of problem-solver. The primary real-world problem that students seem to take up is the problem of getting a degree, and that does little to motivate students to work together in shared problem-solving. Students view knowledge and skills as things to be received rather than constructed and applied. Most of the problems that teachers put to students are Jeroen Merriënboer and Paul Kirschner's "part-task" problems: "highly constructed, well-structured, well-defined, oriented toward the individual, and designed to best fit the content to be taught instead of reality" (2013, 49). While students are sometimes surrounded by faculty who are framing and pursuing questions that address real-world problems, relatively few students are invited into that process. The primary challenge facing most students is to engage well-defined, decontextualized problems that are designed and owned by others. For the most part, students graduate from college not because they have solved local problems but because they have certified their ability to pass classes and move through the educational pipeline.

Drawing on lessons from our visits to Minority-Serving Institutions (MSIs) and innovative programs at other institutions, in the remainder of this chapter we explore an alternative to the traditional curriculum. We describe a curriculum built around students taking on local issues through their participation in a range of opportunities for community engagement and entrepreneurship. Such a curriculum routinely engages students in "whole-task" problems in which they cultivate the skills needed to address problems drawn from the worlds of students, staff, and faculty and their communities. The nature of these problems requires that students join and add value to networks that draw on the diverse perspectives and capabilities of group members. Rather than a series of discipline-based courses, the curriculum becomes a series of linked problem spaces and networks in which students come together and often join with faculty and local communities to engage in real-world problem-solving. Students are challenged to engage in collaborative learning as members of networks that are addressing shared problems.

Build a Curriculum around Local Issues

The idea that schooling should be anchored in real-world problem-solving has been around for a long time. Prioritizing real-world problems over abstract principles was a plank in the agenda of progressive educational reformers of the 1920s. Progressives believed then and now that solving problems by taking on real-world projects engages students in critical analysis rather than rote memorization and leads to deeper learning (National Research Council 2012). Project-based learning has taken stronger root in elementary and secondary education than in higher education; problem-based learning in higher education is used mostly in professional schools. Still, the idea that undergraduate students would be better served by an education rooted in problem-solving is not new. The publication of the Boyer Commission on Educating Undergraduates in the Research University, *Reinventing Undergraduate Education: A Blueprint for America's Research Universities* (1998), placed real-world problem-solving at the center of the contemporary discourse on improving undergraduate education. The Boyer Commission—a group of respected scholars—called attention to the diversity of contemporary college students and campuses and argued that research universities had too often "shortchanged" students by offering them the opportunity to accrue credits and credentials without acquiring "a coherent body of knowledge" (6). Research universities, they argued, needed to trade a focus on learning content, on mastering "The Canon," for learning to use content to engage in inquiry.

The solution that the Boyer Commission proposed was a "radical reconstruction" (6) of undergraduate education at research universities anchored in a "symbiotic relationship between all the participants in university learning that will provide a new kind of undergraduate experience available *only* at research institutions" (7–8). The Boyer Commission called for an "intellectual ecosystem" and "community of learners" that "nurtures exploration and creativity on the part of every member" rather than an "archipelago of intellectual pursuit" (9). The Commission envisioned undergraduate education as providing access to expert researchers, research facilities, and other learners to produce "a particular kind of individual, one equipped with a spirit of inquiry and a zest for problem solving; one possessed of the skill in communication that is the hallmark of clear thinking as well as mastery of language; one informed by a rich and diverse experience. It is that kind of individual that will provide the scientific, technological, academic, political, and creative leadership for the next century" (13).

Their plan? Place "research-based learning"—engaging students in research across their courses with a primary emphasis on interdisciplinary work and original thought—at the center of undergraduate education. To that end, undergraduate education would provide opportunities for collaboration and for practical experiences through fieldwork and internships or activity in "sites of research" (18). Such a curriculum, the Commission suggested, would radically restructure the division of labor in undergraduate education so that students—even first-year students—had mentors who "watch, correct, assist, and encourage" problem-solving and who view diversity and newbies as assets.

The report of the Boyer Commission was at the center of a chorus of turn-of-the-century calls for re-centering undergraduate education. Several other reports extended the Boyer vision beyond research universities, and problem-solving began to take a more central role in the undergraduate curriculum at many institutions (Smith et al. 2004). Before and after the Boyer Commission Report, colleges and universities as different as the University of Delaware, Northwest Arkansas Community College, Sam Houston State University, York College, and Worchester Polytechnic Institute have explored ways to integrate research-based learning and project learning across the curriculum. From among the relatively few institutions that have designed their undergraduate curricula around solving real-world problems, we consider two very different institutions—Olin College and Evergreen State College—to provide sketches of what such a transformation might look like.

A private engineering school located in the Boston metropolitan area, Olin College identifies itself as a "small unique college"

with a selective admissions process. Established in 1998 "to radically change engineering education," Olin refers to the traditional
engineering curriculum as "too narrow": "It teaches students how
to solve problems, but not how to find the right problems to solve,
or how to get their solutions out of the lab and into the world."
The fix is to put the work of engineering—designing solutions to
people's real problems—at the center of the curriculum.

At Olin College, students start their education with required
hands-on engineering classes and complete Design Engineering
and User-oriented Collaborative Design courses in their first
year. Based on a foundation in engineering rather than academic
disciplines outside the field of engineering, students gradually
engage in ever more sophisticated problem-solving in alignment
with their program of study and their own interests. General
education—Arts, Humanities, and Social Sciences—is a program
of study designed to "build strong skills in communication and
contextual awareness" and is supplemented with courses in entrepreneurship in which students develop a "mindset and learn
the tools that are essential to realizing true and sustainable positive change." The general education requirement at Olin allows
students to select additional courses in design and courses focused on their interests. Many courses are completed in studios.
This integrated curriculum guides students toward a capstone
in which they "solve real problems." They choose between the Senior Capstone Program in Engineering (SCOPE), which turns
students into consultants for a company, and an Affordable Design and Entrepreneurship (ADE) initiative, which places students in service of communities to work on lines of inquiry in
such domains as education, environmental quality, and community development.

The program-level college learning outcomes (table 1) at Olin College capture the institution-wide understanding of the meaning of real-world problem-solvers. Olin courses and programs are designed "intentionally" to "instill" in graduates these "key

Table 1. Olin College Program-Level Learning Outcomes

- *Acquire Knowledge, Skills and Approaches.* Build the appropriate breadth and depth of content, techniques and methodologies from diverse fields.
- *Apply Analytical Methods.* Systematically and appropriately apply qualitative, quantitative and critical methodologies and approaches to design experiments, gather data, analyze, model and draw conclusions.
- *Think Critically.* Engage in analyzing, evaluating, synthesizing, and applying diverse information and experiences to support decision-making, attitude formation, action and expression.
- *Develop and Apply Creativity.* Generate novel ideas and approaches, taking into account authentic constraints, that lead to innovative outcomes.
- *Consider Context.* Use a holistic approach that integrates across all relevant contexts and perspectives to identify and address needs and opportunities and consider impacts on individuals, society and environments.
- *Prioritize Sustainability.* Consider the social and environmental systems impacted by engineering and design decisions, aiming for the greatest positive transformation while minimizing unintended negative consequences.
- *Communicate Effectively.* Express meaning successfully through oral, written, and visual media and listen actively to comprehend the meaning of others.
- *Collaborate Successfully.* Create and maintain successful working relationships and identify and resolve interpersonal teaming conflicts to achieve a common goal.
- *Plan and Execute.* Scope, plan and implement projects, maintain accountability for contributions, continuously evaluate progress, navigate uncertainty and adversity, and iterate as needed.
- *Become Self-Directed Learners.* Identify and address learning needs through setting goals, selecting resources and maintaining self-accountability to develop and support intellectual curiosity.
- *Develop Personal and Professional Ethics.* Define and apply one's own beliefs and values to inform one's approaches while considering and respecting the perspectives of others.
- *Foster Identity Development.* Identify and reflect on key moments in life and connect them to the development of one's sense of self.

Source: Olin College of Engineering, Programs of Study and Degree Requirements; Curriculum, Goals, and Outcomes: https://olin.smartcatalogiq.com/en/2017-18/Catalog /Programs-of-Study-and-Degree-Requirements/Curriculum-Goals-and-Outcomes/Learning -outcomes

abilities, skills and mindsets." The first semester at Olin is graded Pass/No record to encourage highly competitive students to focus on learning how to become a person who realizes the college's vision of success rather than on being a person who does what is necessary to get an A. Students' transcripts include grades and GPA as well as a list of their participation in nondegree activities and co-curricular offerings. Student success at Olin College is framed as a record of coming together with others "around common interests" so as "to make a positive impact on the world."

On the other side of the country, Evergreen State College—a public institution—offers a liberal arts education that "prepares students for the way the world happens now, layering academic disciplines so students can focus on how they want to uniquely impact our ever-changing world." Like Olin College, Evergreen invites students to expect a "unique" kind of education, guided by a set of "principles" that are closely aligned with collaborative problem-solving.

Rather than declaring and pursuing a traditional major, students at Evergreen document, reflect on, and update their "intent" through a series of academic statements. In a first-year "orientation essay" they imagine how their education has thus far prepared them to address challenges in the real-world and to spell out "big questions" that have captured their imagination. They begin to pursue their questions through engaging in real-world projects. While Evergreen students take "stand-alone" disciplinary courses beginning their first quarter, their term is typically composed of a single "academic program." The content related to three stand-alone courses is integrated into a single offering. For example, entry-level physics, economics, and history constitute "the Earth Dynamics program." In each program, faculty guide students in developing "tools to navigate real-world issues," sometimes across two or three terms. Rather than grades, students and faculty generate narrative evaluations that "express the thinking that went into your work, what you completed, and the reactions of both you and your faculty members to your work."

The curriculum at Evergreen is designed to provide students with opportunities to fulfill the Six Expectations of an Evergreen Graduate (table 2). Students complete an academic statement each year in which they reflect on their progress, their responsibility for their own learning, and their participation in local communities. While Evergreen offers students "fields of study" that look much like majors in mainstream higher education, these clusters of courses and programs are designed to guide students toward their own "area of emphasis" and, ultimately, to an "individual learning contract" that sets up a capstone—undergraduate research, internships, or independent learning in which students write their own syllabus. In each of their annual statements, students describe the issues they want to take up and the ways in which their education is preparing them to do that real-world work. As students make progress toward degrees, their academic statements map out their education in their "own voice." They articulate the questions that have guided

Table 2. Six Expectations of an Evergreen Graduate

1. Articulate and assume responsibility for your own work.
2. Participate collaboratively and responsibly in our diverse society.
3. Communicate creatively and effectively.
4. Demonstrate integrative, independent, critical thinking.
5. Apply qualitative, quantitative and creative modes of inquiry appropriately to practical and theoretical problems across disciplines.
6. As a culmination of your education, demonstrate depth, breadth and synthesis of learning and the ability to reflect on the personal and social significance of that learning.

Source: Six Expectations of an Evergreen Graduate: https://www.evergreen.edu/about /expectations

their journey, reflect on their learning process, and clarify the goals, "programs," and experiences that they plan to pursue. Their final academic statement becomes part of a student's formal transcript.

Olin College and Evergreen State College are distinctive institutions, and they are as different from one another as together they are different from mainstream higher education. Rather than offering these profiles as models that other institutions could or should emulate, we see these profiles as examples of anchoring a curriculum in problem-solving. Three design principles stand out across these two institutions.

Infusing problem-solving into a curriculum starts with making an explicit departure from the dominant narrative in higher education. Both Olin and Evergreen invite program stakeholders—from students to potential funders—to envision a different kind of undergraduate education. Olin asks students to differentiate the curriculum at "most schools" from Olin's "learning continuum," which offers a "seamless" learning environment in which students are "explorers and creators." Anchored in the assumption that engineering education at many institutions "discourages" many would-be engineers, Olin rebrands engineering education as work on "projects connected to real-world challenges" in which students solve problems for others. In so doing, Olin deemphasizes the dominance of disciplines and majors in favor of creating opportunities for students to frame meaningful questions and design responses. In a similar vein, Evergreen brands itself as a place for students who are inspired by "complexity" in their worlds and are seeking "your way to the world." While students accrue credits that roll up into degrees, the curriculum focuses explicitly on students addressing "real-world issues in all their complexity" and putting "shared learning" to work to engage those issues both as individual learners and through learning with others. Evergreen, the institution asserts, is "a very different place to learn."

A second design principle that Evergreen State College and Olin College share is a tacit commitment to backwards design. They invite students to begin college with a real-world end in mind in designing their pathway through the curriculum to achieve that end. Rather than declaring and identifying with a major, students organize their education around commitments to taking action based on their problem-solving. Evergreen sustains that commitment through annual academic statements and narrative evaluations in which students detail how their experiences in college are reshaping their educational goals and what they are becoming "prepared" to do in the world. Olin invites students into a "profession of innovation" and a curriculum that is focused on educating engineers who address "human and societal needs" with creativity and who create "value through entrepreneurial effort and philanthropy."

First-year design courses and general education courses at Olin include an emphasis on entrepreneurship and guide students toward a final capstone project that puts them in service of a corporation or a community. At both Evergreen and Olin, the expectations of graduates and the tasks that graduates need to be prepared to take up are put front and center at the beginning of the undergraduate experience. Grading policies and graduation requirements position all students to articulate and pursue interests beyond passing classes, and both institutions engage entering students in inquiry that addresses real-world challenges with experts from across disciplines who co-teach courses with other experts. Positioned as facilitators of networks of problem-solvers, faculty routinely collaborate with individuals and small groups on projects. Faculty are expected to engage in professional development that expands their capacity to design the curriculum around issues and to guide students through their projects.

In addition to foregrounding expectations for students about a distinctive education and beginning with the end in mind, Evergreen and Olin have designed curricula that engage students in learning how to learn and how to push projects forward. These capabilities have equal priority with disciplinary knowledge. Both institutions highlight the centrality of interdisciplinary problem-solving, which is embodied in the faculty and reflected in student coursework and their completed projects. The curriculum, both activities and assessments, is built to empower students to participate in networks. Their transcripts document the extent and level of their participation.

Evergreen State College and Olin College are examples of institutions that engage students in addressing shared challenges, yet they also remain committed to building the portfolios of individuals. While collaboration is an important component of these programs, it is positioned as a means to individual learning. The programs in the MSI study seemed to take an additional step, one that institutions not closely tethered to local communities will find difficult. In addition to engaging students with common interests, these programs asked students to connect their interests with local issues and to respond to those issues through class projects, internships, and capstones. This extra step was especially clear at the Tribal Colleges and Universities (TCUs) where students—even students who envisioned careers for themselves that would take them away from the Reservation—often described their success in terms of the success of their Tribe. Again and again TCU students attributed their success and the value of their programs to an education in which they were involved in contributing to the health and well-being of a local community.

This commitment to addressing local issues stood out at Salish Kootenai College (SKC), a college located on the Flathead Indian Reservation in western Montana. The MSI study focused on two programs at SKC: the Department of Academic Success—an interdisciplinary hub responsible for teaching all students at SKC how to be successful in college—and a cluster of science programs that together serve as an informal STEM learning center. Both of these programs put students—all students—to work with staff and faculty in inquiry aimed at addressing local "problems" and sharing their findings. These programs are notable because of the commitments of faculty and staff to "connecting" with students, learning about and from them, and inviting them to contribute to ongoing educational and research initiatives.

Like Evergreen and Olin, SKC brands the college as an explicit departure from traditional higher education. Rather than providing degrees for individuals, the college aims to "empower students to improve the lives of their families and communities through research, leadership and service." In giving expression to this vision of an undergraduate education, the programs we studied at SKC engage students with real-world issues from matriculation through graduation. Students who begin college in remedial math or in calculus are invited to apply for scholarships and internships to become tutors and to help staff and faculty understand what it means for SKC students to succeed in college. Both the Department of Academic Success and the STEM programs define education as project work—such as building robots, measuring water quality in nearby watersheds, and learning note-taking skills—in alignment with the mission of the institution.

Even if they were aware of the distinctive missions of Tribal Colleges and Universities and the mission of SKC in particular, we suspect that many colleges and universities could not easily replicate SKC's mission and practices, for they lack the connection to a people in a place. Still, we see in this TCU a promising approach to anchoring a curriculum in shared problem-solving. This approach starts with an educational purpose that goes beyond individual learning to building and sustaining networks of learners. The SKC institutional vision statement makes explicit the goal of empowering students to problem-solve with respect to where they are going as human beings, and in interview after interview students restated that mission. One student summed it up this way: "what everyone knows is why we are there in the first place. It's for networking and meeting new people and learning." Students described their education in terms of "access" to experts and technology and opportunities to address meaningful issues with others who shared their concern for Indian communities. A science student at SKC emphasized that two elective courses—Native American Women and Indigenous Science—were as important as lab work and math because these courses helped her locate her own commitment to learning science.

Salish Kootenai College defined education as a community good. Keeping all students—including students who begin college in remedial education—engaged in their education, an administrator told us, is "our problem": "Everybody has to understand the needs of students and make changes in teaching styles or whatever it's going to take to help them be successful." A science faculty member mused that his programs grew out of a lab established to "do work for the Tribe." He was proud of a growing number of baccalaureate programs, each of which was linked to local environmental issues and developmental opportunities. At SKC, student success is a community resource; student departure, a community problem.

This widely shared commitment to education as a public good has led students and teachers at SKC to embrace a nontraditional kind of agency. They learn and teach not only as individuals but also as collaborators in networked problem-solving focused on addressing local challenges. The SKC vision—"empowering students to enrich the lives of their families and communities"—seemed to shadow and task the people we interviewed. One student who was about to finish a bachelor's degree and start a job at the Johnson Space Center attributed the launching of his career to a series of networks he had joined through SKC. Early in his degree program, he worked with classmates and a professor to build a robot and, in so doing, learned foundational principles in the field of engineering. That experience deepened his relationship with program faculty and led to internships, first at another TCU and then at the Johnson Space Center in Houston, Texas, where he discovered his passion for engineering. When he returned to SKC, he told faculty: "You have to sign me up. I have to be in this full-time. This is amazing." Reflecting on his path, he attributed his success to mentors who had connected him to educational opportunities that reinforced viewing systems holistically—an education infused with the cultures of the Confederated Tribes of the Flathead Nation. He emphasized that "what I bring to the table" both as a learner and as an engineer is seeing the ways in which systems interact and being willing to facilitate "system integration."

Other students we spoke with at SKC called attention to the ways that the college influenced student agency. As one student put it: "In our directives and our mission statement for the college . . . they definitely emphasize contributing back to your community." Students understood their education as getting and giving back and being supported in contributing to the health of communities. One student spoke of being equipped to go away to graduate school so that she could return and run a lab at SKC; another spoke of being guided first to his GED and then through general education courses so that he could earn a degree in social work and provide the kind of counseling from which he had benefited. These students explicitly linked their success in school to living out practices with which they were "raised": degrees and success came through becoming a writing tutor, building relationships and trust with elders and peers, and developing "cultural knowledge and cultural awareness."

An SKC education is, above all, a space in which students engage in problem-solving on local issues rather than only acquiring disciplinary knowledge and skills and assembling a record of extracurricular activities that prepare them for life after college. The first challenge is graduating Native Americans. Faculty, staff, and students often referred us to the various challenges faced by students who come from under-resourced communities and high schools. Teachers, students told us, have to "know what's going on," and one explained that support services come with "no expectations." Staff listen to what students are working on and customize support. College is first and foremost an opportunity for "networking and meeting new people and learning." As one SKC student elaborated: "One of the best ways I have ever heard it phrased was [that] it is not really who you know; it is how you know them. You can meet all the people in the world, but unless you know them as friends or as colleagues in that kind of a respectful fashion it is not going to do any good for you."

Students we interviewed at SKC often spoke of the challenges of securing funding to stay in school and spending time doing research on local issues. We came to see their education almost as a sequence of "internships." In their studies, students came to recognize what they brought, what experts valued in them, and the ways in which their lives off campus contributed to their participation. Students told us that they found that tutoring others helped them learn and, as importantly, supported the health of their programs. As one student put it: "[Tutoring] reinforces my feeling of contributing something. . . . I think it reinforces my learning by quite a bit." Contributing, they stressed, leads to motivation and confidence. Another student put it this way: "It feels professional, almost. . . . You feel really cool doing these things that these professionals are doing and here we are students, and we are right by their side and we are doing the same experiments as they are."

Salish Kootenai College has created a college campus that is an extension of students' communities, a space for solving problems in the community for the community. SKC faculty design projects with and for local communities. To illustrate, an environmental scientist explained pursuing "issues" that are "directly related to a student that lives in some area where that's an issue that's ongoing at that moment." This principle even grounded his sampling methods: he avoided destructive methods by collecting live insects because that method aligned ethically with students' cultural traditions. Other faculty described developing programs that were linked to employment opportunities on the reservation, even worrying about developing too many programs that aligned with the goals of institutions to which students might transfer rather than with local needs and opportunities. Faculty encouraged students to follow their interests, but they measured educational success mostly in terms of Tribal members working in their fields of study, especially working in their fields of study on the Reservation.

At SKC, the voices of newbies are valued and empowered. Tied to the Flathead Nation, SKC makes space for people from the communities whose problems are being addressed. Faculty and staff spoke candidly about students who were place-bound and were struggling to move through remedial education and into degree programs. Educating their students meant designing programs to validate students' ability to "level up" rather than to certify each student's prior experiences. The undergraduate curriculum was also viewed as a space in which students were able and obligated to contribute. As one student put it:

> It's kind of the seventh-generation way of thinking if you have ever heard of that before. You are not thinking just of yourself but how your actions affect your family seven generations down the line. You have got to leave something for them intact. The way we are kind of living our lives right now. The world at large is not really thinking about how our actions are going to affect the world in 100 years or so, but at tribal colleges and in tribes individually, we are definitely [doing so] . . . . One of the cultural aspects is trying to look how your actions will affect things in the future.

Undergraduate education at SKC was not, she emphasized, "quick." It was about newcomers "finding ways to give back right now."

A curriculum anchored in solving shared real-world problems comes with a commitment to addressing the problems shared across the communities from which students come. This is not to suggest that students do not have the opportunity to pursue their personal interests. They enter a space in which their goals and questions shape and are shaped by the interests of others in the network, novices, experts, and members of different disciplines and communities. Shared interests emerge over time and place as learners and teachers talk about what will sustain and nourish the network. At an institution like SKC, this talk is institutionally mandated but open-ended. The mandate is that networks spend time and energy engaging in spirited dialogue characterized by listening and guided by the assumption that everyone has something to contribute. In the SKC programs in STEM, that talk is fueled and sponsored by a tribe in need of maintaining the environmental, economic, and social health of the community. Degree programs and students come together to serve these shared needs. These STEM programs evolved to respond to students, opportunities, and the needs of local communities.

Framing undergraduate education as taking up, talking through, and responding to local issues changes the game. Students are recognized as human beings who contribute, and the curriculum provides them with real-world opportunities to work together on local issues and also positions them to envision the potential impact of their contributions. Teaching and academic support are designed to fuel and inform meaningful action. In the next two sections, we explore two features of an education that is focused on responding to local issues: community-engagement and entrepreneurship. Students who work on shared problems collaborate with local communities in addressing real-world issues facing these communities by putting resources to work in new ways in order to create value both for students and communities.

Create Opportunities for Community-Engaged Learning

Community engagement in higher education is well traveled but also contentious territory. The narrative goes something like this: American colleges and universities are social institutions that have variously engaged and served communities. More often than not, they have done so selectively, usually exclusively. From the founding of Harvard College in 1636 to the middle of the twentieth century, relatively few Americans attended college and many citizens—people of color, women, Jews, working-class students—were systematically excluded. The aims of the Morrill Act (1862) notwithstanding, curricular and research agendas were set on campus and, more often than not, local communities were not directly involved. Undergraduate education—especially baccalaureate education—remained an "elite" system (Trow 1970). Things began to change in the middle of the twentieth century. Funding for research following World War II, the GI Bill, and the Civil Rights movement opened what Ernest Boyer (1996) described near the close of the twentieth century as "an absolutely spectacular experiment": colleges and universities "joined" American society "in a cultural commitment to rising expectations—and what was for most (not all) GIs a privilege became for their children and grandchildren an absolute right. And there's no turning back" (20). While faculty have often questioned demands for universal access and applied research, there has been no turning back.

The American experiment with mass higher education has put colleges and universities under pressure from within and outside to engage increasingly diverse students and their communities (Boyer 1990; Newman 1985). This pressure increased in the 1970s and 1980s due to growing discontent with the market-centered orientation of undergraduate education at many institutions and concerns about the civic disengagement of many students (Levine 1980). The Campus Outreach Opportunity League (1984) and the Campus Compact (1985) encouraged institutions to place more emphasis on educating students for citizenship through opportunities such as service learning and volunteering. From the 1980s forward, colleges and universities have hosted hundreds of projects and initiatives and campus service-learning centers supported by diverse federal funding sources, dedicated journals, a Carnegie classification for "community engagement" (2005), the designation of "anchor institutions," a national taskforce (2009), and the advancement of student learning outcomes related to civic engagement.

While there remains some uncertainty as to whether community-engaged institutions have been genuinely "engaged" in problem-solving in local communities (Kellogg Commission on the Future of State and Land-Grant Universities 1999) or cultivating democratic citizens (Talloires Network 2005), the call for colleges and universities to engage with their respective communities remains largely unchallenged (Butin 2012; National Task Force on Civic Learning and Democratic Engagement 2012). Developing a curriculum that provides students with community-engaged learning experiences has been found to deepen student learning (Bringle and Hatcher 2009; Eyler and Giles 1999). It can also position students to learn from, with, and for others. Through formal and informal opportunities to engage in shared endeavors aimed at addressing challenges facing communities, students can learn to draw on the skills and knowledge of participants and, in so doing, learn how to become collaborative learners.

The MSIs study drove home for us the link between community engagement and collaborative learning. While each of the institutions in the study sought to make college relevant to the minoritized communities they sought to serve, it was the Full Circle Project at Sacramento State University that helped us to make the connection between community engagement and collaborative learning. The Full Circle Project was developed in part to ensure that Asian American and Pacific Islander (AAPI) students who successfully complete their first year of college not only persist to a degree but are also "empowered" to participate in communities both on campus and off campus. As they complete a sequence of courses in ethnic studies and participate in a leadership program and community-based learning experiences, students host public discussions of contemporary issues on campus. Many become involved with local schools and community organizations including the 65th Street Corridor Project—a community development project that includes a partnership with seventh through twelfth grade schools in which students mentor low-income and ethnically diverse middle school students (Conrad and Gasman 2015, 226).

Faculty involved in the Full Circle Project emphasized that beyond providing student support, the project has embraced a "vision" of undergraduate education that "connects students with their own histories" and provides them with opportunities to "actualize" an "understanding of their role in society and their role in social change." Graduates, as one faculty member put it, "really walk the walk" and leave college with "a concrete vision" of what it means to make use of an education in a local community because their program contributed to a series of endeavors. These endeavors included helping to establish an archive of Asian-American history, tutoring in after-school programs, establishing an Asian American film festival, and hosting dialogues about the needs of communities both on and off campus. Students explained to us that participation in the program forced them out of their "comfort zone." Rather than answering questions posed by teachers, they listen to and learn from group members and community members and then represent what they are learning in ethnic studies classes in ways that motivate rooms full of faculty or sixth graders or community members or Sacramento State undergraduates. Students envision being educated as becoming a community activist.

The Full Circle Project embeds in undergraduate students a commitment to creating and sustaining reciprocal relationships with local communities along with developing the capabilities that students need to address local problems. Through this program and others, Sacramento State has become one of many institutions at which pursuing an undergraduate education comes with the requirement to learn what democratic community engagement involves and why it matters as well as embracing the obligation to work in two-way relationships with local communities to address real-world problems (Butin 2012; National Task Force on Civic Learning and Democratic Engagement 2012; Saltmarsh, Hartley, and Clayton 2009).

While we see this kind of community-engaged learning with local communities as a promising path to collaborative learning, unlike Ernest Boyer and many others we do not view the ongoing experiment with community-engaged higher education as reclaiming some historic civic commitment. Rather, we believe that engaging diverse students in an increasingly diverse democracy confronts colleges and universities with a new "experiment," one that challenges their historic social charter. Community engagement takes undergraduate education beyond having faculty, students, and campuses pursue their individual agendas off-campus; instead, the call is to align their agendas, programs, and learning experiences with the needs of communities through collaboration. This requires participants to reject engrained deficit views of novices and non-academics and to recognize students and community members as full partners who together conduct research and solve problems. Rather than focusing primarily on delivering knowledge, community-engaged faculty members curate resources and opportunities for networks of learners to cultivate ideas for addressing real-world problems. In so doing, assessment as the rank ordering of students on opaque performance standards gives way to collecting information about what students do with their learning in new situations (for example, in interdisciplinary courses and in the field) and using that information to guide the improvement of instruction and student learning as well as the solving of local problems.

This experiment is, of course, already well underway in American undergraduate education. Many American colleges and universities provide rich and compelling examples of community engagement and community-based learning programs. We draw on two well-documented programs—the Bonner Program and the University Studies program at Portland State University—as examples of community-engaged learning, including ways in which they contribute to an undergraduate education driven by collaborative learning.

Established by the Corella & Bertram F. Bonner Foundation, the Bonner Program aims at providing "access to education, opportunity to serve." The founding president was Wayne Meisel, whose 1984 "walk for action" and Campus Outreach Opportunity League were drivers of the civic engagement movement in American higher education. Since its founding in 1989, the Bonner Foundation has seeded a series of projects that have encouraged and helped shape community engagement on college and university campuses. The institutions that host the Bonner Program have become a network through which a sophisticated approach to community-engaged learning has developed. Since the founding of the Bonner Foundation, the enduring goal of the Bonner Program has been to "transform students, communities, and campuses through service."

The Bonner Program that recruits, trains, and supports Bonner Scholars and self-funded Bonner Leaders illustrates a path to community-engaged undergraduate education. The Program values community engagement and sustains a commitment to service, recruiting students with high needs and "an ethic for service" and providing Scholars with four years of support to participate in an intensive "community engagement opportunity." This "inclusive and integrative" approach to "civic learning and community engagement" seeks to get past "disjointed co-curricular community engagement" and instead to develop a network of students that makes community engagement the centerpiece of an undergraduate education (figure 1). Bonner Scholars and Leaders participate in the Program and work with community partners— often a single partner—for their entire undergraduate education, including summer internships. This developmental model moves through stages from joining the program and "getting to know yourself" to "leaving a legacy" and living a life of commitment (table 3). Across these stages, the Bonner Program cultivates a set of commitments that define students' education: community building; diversity; civic engagement; social justice; global perspective, and spiritual exploration. Students who complete the Program invest the equivalent of one year of full-time employment in a community of practice engaged with local issues.

The Bonner Program explicitly rejects the idea that "Bonners"— as Scholars and Leaders are called inside the Program—receive

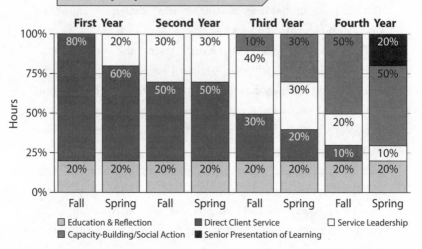

Personally responsible citizen

Participatory citizen

Social justice citizen

Bonner Program Four-Year Student Development Model
Source: "Bonner Program Model," by the Bonner Program, 2020, http://www.bonner
.org/bonner-program-model

financial support in exchange for volunteering. Instead, the Program provides students who are already committed to community engagement with opportunities to collaborate with network schools by providing "integrative educational and experiential pathways, and the structures that support them." The Program guides the 30 to 100 Bonners on each campus through a sequence of experiences that include long-term placement in a community site. Students in the Program enter a network in which they spend 8–10 hours each week in "training, education, and reflection" as well as direct service. Their campus provides curricular and co-curricular opportunities to develop the knowledge, skills, and

Table 3. Bonner Program Training and Education Themes

	Semester	Training and Education Theme	Sample Workshop Modules
1st Year	Fall	Getting to Know Yourself, Each Other, and Your Place	Identity Circles, An Introduction to Place, Community Asset Mapping
	Spring	Solutions-Oriented Community Engagement	Discovering What Works, Measuring Impact, Attacking Root Causes, Cultivating Collaborations
2nd Year	Fall	Leading Groups	Planning Effective Meetings, Introduction to Effective Facilitation
	Spring	Knowing Your Issue	Researching the Scope of a Local Problem, Leading an Issue-Focused Discussion/Forum
3rd Year	Fall	Managing Projects	Overview of Project Management, Analyzing Project Requirements, Executing and Evaluating a Project
	Spring	Managing Organizations	Understanding the Public Sector, Assessing and Building Organizational Capacity, Finding Your Vocation
4th Year	Fall	Leaving a Legacy	Preparing a Leadership Transition, Public Speaking and Presentations of Learning, Finding Your Vocational Fit
	Spring	Lives of Commitment	Interviewing Skills, Life after Bonner-Staying Well and Engaged

Source: Adapted from the Bonner Foundation. *Training, Education & Reflection*. 2019–2020: http://www.bonner.org/education-and-reflection

attributes that students need to participate and contribute in community-engagement work.

As a full partner in these pathways, the Bonner Program does more than provide funding for students. The Bonner Program 2019 Strategic Plan tethers strengthening student pathways and building "campus-wide community engagement" to transforming American higher education. As part of this effort, the Program facilitates the Bonner Network of institutions and collaborations with organizations like the AAC&U to operate campus centers; support staff and faculty development; design community-engaged pathways through which institutions can develop alternative majors; and develop and disseminate research on community engagement, curriculum, and learning outcomes. An online Bonner Learning Community was launched in 2020 to support ongoing training and dialogue within the network. Since 1997, the Bonner Foundation has promoted community-based research as "a form of community engagement in which community-identified needs for knowledge and information are addressed through partnerships often involving students, faculty, and community organizations or groups." This longstanding commitment has led to a networked group of issues-based partnerships that promote social change. Beyond serving local communities, Bonners are engaged in producing policy research, "a strategy that mobilizes college students to research and share policy research with their community partners and with other students." The Bonner curriculum includes training in how to work with community partners to change policies and implement projects, and some campuses offer a "community engagement course model" that provides Bonners a chance to join or launch a social action campaign to change a public or institutional policy.

As the Bonner Foundation moves into its fourth decade, it exemplifies a "community of practice" distributed across colleges and universities and their community partners (Hoy, Johnson, and Hackett 2012). This network is supported by a web-based reporting system, a set of shared strategic initiatives, campus centers, cohorts of students, faculty development support, issue-based national partnerships, and a process through which partners can make requests for "capacity-building projects and academic research." In a 2013 publication, founding president

Meisel offered three reasons for the effectiveness of the Bonner network of institutions. First, the network embraces collaboration: "we have not imported anything to the institutions with which we collaborate" (xi). Rather than establishing "Bonner schools" (xii), the Program promotes educational pathways that help institutions—colleges and universities and also community organizations—realize their missions. Second, the focus of the Bonner Program has remained on helping campus staff to develop teams of student leaders who implement the Program. Third, as Meisel put it, "we have never claimed success" (xiii). The Bonner Program is invested in sustaining partnerships that engage local issues as they emerge rather than achieving a designated level of market saturation or a designated rate of student graduation.

The Bonner Programs offer a snapshot of a comprehensive approach to providing undergraduates with formal and informal opportunities for community-engaged learning through a network of institutions. The University Studies Program at Portland State University (PSU) provides an example of how this kind of programming can find expression in an institution. A former participant in the Bonner AmeriCorps Program, PSU is a self-acknowledged urban university, an institution where in the 1990s students chose the motto "let knowledge serve the city" and where three presidents were engaged for almost 30 years in building and sustaining relationships between the university and the city. Judith Ramaley (1990–1997) codified the mission of an urban university as the responsibility "(1) to find a means to link learning and community life through the design of the curriculum, and (2) to serve as a center and resource for community building on the community's terms" (2001, 15). Daniel Bernstine (1997–2007) elaborated on this vision for PSU: "My vision is of a university so thoroughly engaged with its community . . . that people throughout the region refer to it as 'our university,' [that] PSU is recognized as a national leader in community-based learning and research strategies that provide meaningful opportunities for students and faculty to address complex issues in diverse communities locally and worldwide" (quoted in Kecskes, Kerrigan, and Patton 2006, 51).

Wim Wiewel (2007–2017) carried forward this vision and challenged PSU to become an "anchor institution" by establishing an executive-level Office of Strategic Partnerships and opening a "front door for community engagement" (Flynn 2015, 160). Undergraduate education is at the center of PSU's commitment to community engagement. Under President Ramaley, faculty redesigned the general education program in the early 1990s as faculty members became involved in campus-wide discussions of how to better support students as learners and how to transform general education from the transmission of facts to the cultivation of lifelong learners (Kecskes, Kerrigan, and Patton 2006). The result—the University Studies Program—is general education that is aligned with theories of adult education and the needs of a place (Reitenauer, Draper-Beard, and Schultz 2018). University Studies challenges students "to think holistically, care deeply, and engage courageously in imagining and co-creating a just world." By 2020, that work was scaffolded in a curriculum that is inclusive, interdisciplinary, inquiry-based, and

- provokes students to build self-efficacy through relational learning across differences;
- encourages a community of educators to practice engaged teaching for transformative learning,; and
- advances civic engagement, reflective practice, and the scholarship of teaching and learning.

As with the Bonner Programs, community engagement is embedded throughout undergraduate education at PSU. Freshman Inquiry (FRINQ) is a year-long sequence of courses on themes such as connections between humans and nature; the city of Portland as a context for human development; the history and sociology of race along with the biology that undermines the concept; sustainability; the role that art plays in a life in Portland; the generation of stories of power and perception; and the impact of health, communities, and human rights on human happiness. Each FRINQ sequence is designed to provide students with opportunities to take on local problems, and the FRINQ "learning objectives" emphasize problem-solving, inquiry, and life-long learning: "When students complete Freshman Inquiry, they will be expected to be able to apply writing, quantitative literacy, speech, visual/graphic skills, and current information technologies to problems requiring analysis and discovery. Freshman Inquiry will prepare students to move on to increasingly rigorous and sophisticated levels of inquiry, with the skills and habits of mind necessary for academic success and life-long learning in a society where the ability to think across disciplinary boundaries is increasingly required." Sections are co-taught and emphasize student-led discussions and project-based learning: each section guides students in developing an electronic portfolio. Each FRINQ is supported by required mentored-inquiry sections in which 12 students work together with a peer mentor—a PSU undergraduate or graduate student—"to understand and apply material from the main class session." In 2007, 80 percent of FRINQ students engaged in community-based learning.

The community engagement introduced in FRINQ is carried forward by Sophomore Inquiry (SINQ), the next requirement in the University Studies Program. SINQ organizes thematically linked, interdisciplinary clusters of three general education courses that introduce students to disciplinary concepts and methods they will use in upper division clusters. Each of the three courses explores one SINQ topic in detail with continued mentor session support. The list of SINQ course topics reads like a list of contemporary community issues: community studies; design thinking; freedom, privacy, and technology; interpreting the past; and leading social change. SINQ leads to an Upper Division Cluster, three to four disciplinary courses that introduce innovative ways of approaching community issues. In these courses, students assume greater responsibility for putting knowledge and skills to work on the Cluster issue. Mentor sessions give way to web-based information and program and cluster advisors.

The first three years of University Studies sets up the Senior Capstone in which students join an ongoing "community project," "applying all you've learned" (Kerrigan 2015). These projects range from assisting in foreign language education for young children in Portland area schools to working on sustainability projects at Sunnyside Environmental School to joining programs in various city and state agencies and institutions or ongoing projects around the world. Small groups of students work as teams, studying with a faculty expert, conducting their own research, advancing community-based projects, and presenting their results. The entire journey is documented by students as they learn the methods and policies in play at their community site, practice the process of reflection through FRINQ assignments, and then decide how to document their learning as they move through the program.

What are the outcomes of this program? While students use the language of service to describe their experience, they are part of a program that is collaborating with local communities. The assessment of the capstone that was included in the 2014–2015 University Studies Annual Assessment Report provides a snapshot of the program (Carpenter 2015). In that report, students identified positive learning outcomes such as "increased capacity for communicating and collaborating across difference, appreciation of the diversity of persons within our shared communities, integration of content knowledge (around, for example, water systems, incarceration, and organ donation), and understanding of one's responsibility to engage in pro-civic behavior." Student evaluations confirmed that many participate in what Judith Ramaley (2001) referred to as a "fully realized university-community relationship":

> a common agenda and sharing of both power and responsibility as
> well as risk and reward; (2) an ability to share power and resources
> equitably with the community; (3) the creation of extraordinary
> community-based/service-learning opportunities for students in
> ways that require faculty and administrators to be equally open
> and responsive to the interests and concerns of their students and
> of the community; and (4) the inclusion of community concerns as
> a legitimate set of expectations about what the legitimate goals and
> successful outcomes of a community-university partnership or
> engagement will be (13).

Faculty assessment of portfolios composed of syllabi, assignment descriptions, and examples of student work have consistently found that students find ways to apply disciplinary knowledge to local issues in this aligned curriculum.

Both the Bonner Programs and the PSU University Studies Program outline ways in which community-engaged education can scaffold collaborative learning. Both programs revise the dominant pathway through college from a collection of courses that make up a major to a set of required experiences through which students take increasing responsibility for applying knowledge and skills from multiple disciplines to local issues. For many students, these programs transform undergraduate education from credits and requirements to collaborative inquiry focused on local issues. Both programs create space and rewards for faculty to work across disciplines and develop integrated pathways through college that are focused on local issues and on cultivating the skills and knowledge that students need to address these issues. They locate and support opportunities to learn in classrooms and in local communities where instructors and students alike learn from, with, and for others.

This vision of what it means to be a "learner" and where and how that learning happens repositions students across the undergraduate experience. Students become agents who are asked to articulate the ways in which fulfilling educational requirements prepares them to work on local problems and build their problem-solving capabilities. Their education requires that they develop and reflect on their ability to guide their inquiry and contribute to ongoing projects. In the Bonner Programs, doing policy research and writing policy is becoming part of an undergraduate education; a PSU education integrates general education learning outcomes with participation in community-based teams. Rather than simply picking up credentials, undergraduates in these programs work on shared problems in which they learn how to contribute. They are learning to be collaborative learners, people who co-teach, co-learn, and contribute on and off campus.

These programs have the potential to transform institutions into places where collaborative learning is expected. Bonner Foundation funding supports local student and faculty leaders and links institutions in a network through which the curriculum, professional development, and research are closely aligned. In establishing the University Studies Program, PSU has made funding available to individual faculty and to departments to reimagine courses and programs in collaboration with their local communities. Bonners and every PSU University Studies student are expected to tether their education to local communities. Student engagement with local communities routinely triggers program support for incremental curriculum development as well as faculty professional development and the cultivation of community partnerships. These two community-engagement networks reward the development of relevant expertise by both faculty and staff. At PSU, the development of required courses provides opportunities for faculty to teach differently and to rewrite departmental mission statements that highlight community partnerships. The Bonner Pipeline Project invests in the development of community-engagement professionals and the renewal of their vision of community and civic-engaged learning and education. Bonners have created a network of Bonner schools, places where community engagement is part of the undergraduate experience. These programs make the collaborative pursuit of promising ideas business-as-usual in undergraduate education.

One way that these programs are transforming undergraduate education is through recalibrating what counts as student success. While these programs count the number of students who persist and complete their degrees, they gather two other kinds of data. They measure the number of students involved with local organizations, and they assess students' community engagement by collecting student reflections, capstone presentations, and stakeholder feedback. Along with the academic progress of students, an important measure of students' educational success is time and energy spent in collaborative inquiry in which staff and students develop back-and-forth relationships with local communities aimed at addressing local challenges. By tracking community engagement, these programs have come to view educational success in part by the quality of civic learning across the program and the engagement of local communities and issues through, for example, the number of elementary students tutored, community-based websites that are published and updated, policy briefs written, and public meetings facilitated.

In summary, undergraduate education that is anchored in solving shared problems is community-engaged. It cultivates and sustains networks that are engaged in collaborative research and development with local communities on and off campus and ties both institutional and student success to the success of networks taking on real-world problems.

Provide Opportunities for Students, Staff, and Faculty to Practice Entrepreneurship

Early in our conversations with students and faculty in the MSIs study, we recognized that they often linked success in college to becoming better equipped to solve problems facing their families and their communities. As a San Diego City College (SDCC) student who was a peer mentor in the First-Year Experience (FYE) program put it, he and his peers were finding their "route" to "becoming role models." He explained that success in college for him and most students in the FYE program was not a sure thing. He was returning to college four years after his first attempt, and his route to success was mediated by "family drama that was going on in the household, financial issues . . . all of those come into play." His route started with a "guardian angel": his cousin who was completing a degree challenged him to reflect on educational goals that would not only pay off for him but also empower him to "help others," that is, to be a role model.

This student determined that to become a role model his education had to have value both in the workplace and in his home community. While that led him to identify a target industry and profession along with a fall back, it was the SDCC First-Year Experience program that got him moving. He checked off the "habits" he had acquired: time management, community engagement, self-presentation, self-reflection, curiosity, and grit. In addition to habits that obliged him to approach college differently, the program required him to "network," find "good friends" and "get active with faculty" so that he could innovate when a work promotion fell through or he broke his arm or he faced a required course that "bored" him. These new habits and practices, he emphasized, empowered him to "maintain" educational progress while he held three jobs.

The first-year experience at San Diego City College—especially student support services and first-year English, math, and general education courses—was designed to promote this type of educational innovation. Peer mentors, academic advisors, and faculty described the program as an incubator in which students practiced using existing networks to find new ways to address challenges on and off campus. Nearly all of the institutions in the MSI study were engaged in this kind of innovation. They incorporated internships into the first year of the curriculum and took students on off-campus trips with the expectation that students would bring new ideas about what college was about, how they could get through college, and how they could use their college education to contribute back to their home communities.

To prepare students to take on local issues, programs in the MSI study often went beyond well-established boundaries in mainstream higher education. They invited students and their teachers to view themselves as educational innovators. They seemed to expect students, staff, and faculty to become J. Gregory Dees's (2001) social entrepreneurs:

- Adopting a mission to create and sustain social value;
- Recognizing and relentlessly pursuing new opportunities to serve that mission;
- Engaging in a process of continuous innovation, adaptation, and learning;
- Acting boldly without being limited by resources currently in hand; and
- Exhibiting heightened accountability to the constituencies served and for the outcomes created.

Programs in the MSIs study embraced various innovative practices that remixed traditional education programs and resources to advance student success. Faculty and staff at Chief Dull Knife College (CDKC) broke apart the developmental math curriculum by designing new classrooms, changing the sequence and length of courses, and transforming traditional faculty loads. At both CDKC and SDCC, math faculty described taking the risk of not covering new content in the first week of the class so that teachers and students could co-construct their classroom roles and develop a shared stake in learning math together.

This approach to education is not about educating heroic entrepreneurs or making undergraduate education pay off solely in financial terms. Rather, the emphasis is on exploring new ways to use limited resources to support the development of all students. In so doing, the MSIs placed major emphasis on empowering networks to promote the educational success of traditionally underrepresented students who had been poorly served in mainstream higher education and, no less, networks that take on local issues. Students in the programs wanted degrees and knowledge and skills that they could roll over into jobs and income; their engagement in real-world problem-solving needed to pay off in completed classes and marketable experiences. But because they found themselves in programs that supported collaborative problem-solving, they saw educational value as including the development of knowledge and skills that helped others to learn and also helped the networks in which they were involved in making progress in solving local problems. Students spoke over and over about coming to see their education differently, including the place of technology, their peers, and their teachers.

The idea that entrepreneurship has a place in undergraduate education is not new. Courses in entrepreneurship date to at least the end of World War II, and 5,000 courses were offered across the country by 2008 (Ewing Marion Kauffman Foundation 2013, 1). Indeed, there is a growing consensus that American higher education in the twenty-first century should become more entrepreneurial (Cohen and Kisker 2010; Thelin and Others 1988). In a period that is defined by what Burton Clark (1998) labeled "disquieting turmoil," colleges and universities are being pushed and pulled to innovate in response to the demands of students, evolving knowledge-based enterprises, and government calls for help on social and economic challenges. Institutions that are changing their organization and practices in order to flourish in this fast-changing environment, Clark argued, are not only "innovative" but "entrepreneurial." Two decades ago, Clark analyzed a set of institutions that were deliberately changing the ways in which they did business from the bottom up without losing sight of "academic legitimacy" (4). These universities chose to explore and experiment with how they respond to internal and external demands. They sensed that in fast-moving times the prudent course of action is to be out front, shaping the impact of demands made upon them, steering instead of drifting (5).

Burton Clark's five elements of transformation—a strengthened steering core, an expanded developmental periphery, a diversified funding base, a stimulated academic heartland, and an integrated entrepreneurial culture—were offered as a recipe for institutional change. We see them as a recipe for institutions that are ready to promote collaborative learning. An entrepreneurial institution is willing to respond, and respond quickly, to "expanding and changing demands" (5). Rather than holding on to "old university boundaries," entrepreneurial institutions reach across traditional boundaries—frameworks, disciplines, departments, roles, domains of activity—and recruit into short- and long-term networks the knowledge, skills, and relationships needed to seize on new opportunities. These networks are composed of and steered by faculty, staff, and students who step over traditional boundaries to work on shared problems (sometimes with "discretionary funds") in cultures that fuse a willingness to change with established values, beliefs, and practices. In becoming entrepreneurial, institutions can become spaces for collaborative problem-solving.

Clark documented the ways in which a set of European institutions became entrepreneurial but had little to say about what that kind of transformation might mean for American undergraduate education. We turn to the Kauffman Campuses Initiative (2003–2013) to explore what it might mean to make the undergraduate experience more entrepreneurial. Starting in 2003 with funding from the Kauffman Initiative, 19 campuses experimented with infusing entrepreneurship into a variety of programs, including programs at the undergraduate level. In framing the initiative, the Kauffman Panel on Entrepreneurship in Higher Education—a group of scholars that advised the initiative—emphasized that "college learning must teach students how to make sense of and how to affect the reality in which they will actually live" (Kauffman Panel on Entrepreneurship in Higher Education 2008, 4). They emphasized that education cannot succeed if it becomes insular and static. Along with studying "great works" of the past and longstanding questions about human nature, the Panel stressed that a distinctive strength of American higher education also should be dynamism and adaptability, a capacity to address urgent, current questions of nature, society, and human experience as well as classic ones (4). It concluded that "entrepreneurship and a college education are inextricably bound to one another," "entrepreneurship is a dominant force in the contemporary America," and higher education makes innovation and improvement "intelligible" (4).

From the standpoint of the Kauffman Panel, entrepreneurship is a "subject" and an approach to institutional management as well as "a pervasive approach to learning" (4). Through general education and majors, the aim is "the entrepreneurial move from intelligibility to innovation" (12): an undergraduate education infused with entrepreneurship can guide students to learn to innovate and apply new ideas to create a "sustainable future" (15). Entrepreneurship in higher education "cannot be restricted" to the world of commerce. Instead, entrepreneurship is viewed as a social process of transformation and value creation, and the Panel and campuses agreed that making entrepreneurship integral to a college education requires doing more than offering more business-oriented courses and co-curricular experiences.

The Kauffman Campuses adapted and implemented this vision of entrepreneurship in ways that made sense locally. Individual essays from each campus summarize the impact of this initiative as well as identify various applications of Kauffman funding. The campuses introduced interdisciplinary courses, certificates, and programs in entrepreneurship outside of business and engineering schools. They hosted lectures, panels, interviews, and fellowships that brought entrepreneurs to campus, and they established business incubators, competitions and fellowships through which students and faculty develop commercial and nonprofit ventures. Nearly all of the campuses funded faculty professional development and student scholarships to motivate engagement in entrepreneurship. The essays from each campus also indicate that institutions often wrestle with whether to infuse entrepreneurship throughout the institution or provide a focused experience for fewer students, and how to balance teaching about entrepreneurship and opportunities for students to engage in entrepreneurial practices.

To illustrate how entrepreneurship has been woven into the undergraduate experience through the Kauffman Campus Initiative, we look at how two institutions—Wake Forest University and Arizona State University (ASU)—transformed their programs and practices through participation in the initiative. As they entered the initiative, both ASU and Wake Forest embraced an inclusive "view of entrepreneurship." ASU built on the idea of "Value Entrepreneurship" that was already embedded in the institution's vision of itself as a "New American University": a comprehensive public research university redesigning itself to include all members of its local communities and advance the "discovery of public value" and to be responsible for "the economic, social, cultural and overall health of the communities it serves." Since entrepreneurship was already explicit in the ASU mission and vision statements, ASU used Kauffman funding to further integrate an existing commitment to building public value into outreach materials and other official documents (Arizona State University 2012).

At Wake Forest, entrepreneurship and its connection to wealth creation were initially viewed as contradicting a liberal arts education aimed at cultivating "a critical appreciation of moral values, as well as applying and using knowledge in the service of humanity" (Torrance 2013, 3). Early in the initiative an interdisciplinary team met weekly for a semester to arrive at a workable definition of entrepreneurship: "the process through which individuals and groups take advantage of their knowledge and resources to identify and pursue opportunities, initiate change and create sustainable value in their lives and the lives of others" (4). This definition resonated with the long-standing Wake Forest motto of *Pro Humanitate*. Engaging in entrepreneurship was seen as another way of realizing the campus commitment "to make a difference in the world."

At both ASU and Wake Forest, the alignment between an inclusive definition of entrepreneurship and their institutional missions and cultures paved the way for faculty and students to learn about and practice entrepreneurship. While both institutions found students and faculty open to engaging in entrepreneurship broadly defined, most faculty and students outside schools of business and engineering knew little about entrepreneurship and had not thought about how an undergraduate education might be enriched by becoming more entrepreneurial. In reflecting on the process of becoming more entrepreneurial, Wake Forest recognized the need for "greater creativity and willingness to try innovative approaches on the part of students" and the exploitation of "fertile areas for possible innovation and creativity . . . at the boundaries between disciplines" that too few students and faculty had heretofore inhabited (Torrance 2013, 4). ASU surveys of students and general education faculty at the start of the project produced similar findings.

Wake Forest and ASU made entrepreneurship more visible through communication programs, university-level offices, funding faculty champions, and incentives for student engagement. Both institutions also developed new curricula. Wake Forest started with freestanding workshops that became credit-bearing courses and then a minor composed of three required courses (Innovation and Creativity, Foundations of Entrepreneurship, and Managing the Entrepreneurial Venture: Startup to Early Growth) and three elective courses (Thought and Behavior, Leadership and Engaging the World, and Entrepreneurial Process). Arizona State University funded the development of interdisciplinary courses and departments across the institution to teach students "to develop and implement ideas that solve challenges" and also meet degree requirements. An entrepreneurship curriculum was infused into ASU 101, a course required of all ASU students and taught across schools and colleges. In this course, ASU students are introduced at the beginning of their education to the Value Entrepreneurship and opportunities for learning about and engaging in entrepreneurship.

These curricular initiatives at Wake Forest and ASU were accompanied by structured opportunities for community-based learning within and outside of credit-bearing courses. ASU established a set of interrelated and independent "pipelines" that guide students from across the curriculum into entrepreneurial activities. This process began by bringing University Innovation Fellows to campus for a year to transform programs and practices and led to revising websites and communication practices and establishing physical and virtual centers. In turn, a range of opportunities for students to become entrepreneurs were knit into undergraduate education at ASU. Competitions and venture funding became front-page news and were highlighted by advisors and the Career Center. Changemaker Central provided physical space on all ASU campuses in which students and community organizations could connect with a Change Agent and learn about joining or starting ventures. 10,000 students, faculty, and community members used a web-based platform named 10,000 Solutions to propose solutions to identified local "challenges" and find others with whom to collaborate. A smaller campus, Wake Forest already supported venture competitions and for-credit as well as stipend internships. Kauffman funding enabled the university to expand its Center for Entrepreneurship that houses coaches and mentors, the Minor in Entrepreneurship, and a variety of co-curricular programs through which students can build their skills and enhance their knowledge base, find ongoing enterprises, and find support for launching their own ventures—including a year-long fellowship in which students develop and launch social enterprises (Gatewood, Conner, and West 2012).

Being a Kauffman Campus has had a significant impact at both Wake Forest and ASU. To begin, both institutions have found that the emphasis on entrepreneurship has led to an increased emphasis on teaching what one Wake Forest faculty member labeled "skills of public engagement" along with "creativity, boldness, experimentation, and an acute awareness of the dynamics of innovation and team collaboration." Moreover, both campuses came to recognize that infusing their curriculum with entrepreneurship could strengthen existing programs and initiatives including "community-relevant projects" and opportunities for students to apply what they are learning to local issues. Becoming more entrepreneurial also deepened networks on and off campus. A faculty member at Wake Forest put it this way:

> The initiative opened my eyes to two things. First, students did
> not need to put their dreams on hold during the four years they
> attended college. Second, professors have a unique ability to act as
> entrepreneurs and catalysts for student entrepreneurship. By
> working with other participants in the Kauffman initiative, my
> trajectory as an assistant professor was radically reshaped. I left
> the "publish or perish" mentality by the wayside and adopted a
> "partner for productivity" strategy as a teacher-scholar. Before
> joining the initiative, I worked on my own research projects and
> my own classes. Since teaching my first initiative-sponsored class,
> I have launched three companies, been more active as a biotech
> consultant, and have started a new branch of research that has
> nearly doubled the external grant dollars coming into my lab. My

productivity in terms of publications is higher, but my real productivity is measured by the joy I have in seeing things of value created through partnerships. (Torrance 2013, 22)

Through the integration of entrepreneurship into undergraduate education at the Kauffman Campuses, real-world problem-solving has become a centerpiece of the undergraduate curriculum. In addition to providing opportunities for community engagement, Wake Forest and ASU ask students, staff, and faculty to take responsibility for becoming problem-solvers who can identify and pursue promising ways to build value with and for others. These campuses are seeking to educate citizens who have the capacities to develop innovative approaches to solving problems and capitalizing on opportunities.

Tied to community engagement, the focus on collaboratively creating value seems to us to be an invitation to learn from, with, and for others. Yet, while entrepreneurship can serve as an entrée into collaborative learning, the education of individual entrepreneurs need not. The initiatives at Wake Forest and ASU suggest to us that the key is the way in which "value" is defined and understood. As we scroll through the growing literature on social entrepreneurship, we are struck by the continued focus on boosting heroic entrepreneurs and privatizing resources and services. Much of this literature draws a bright line between economic value—often rendered as financial value or market value—and social value as though somehow economies, political and otherwise, sit outside societies. In much of what we read, value is reified. There is little explanation of how different kinds of value—financial rewards, social benefits, cultural resources, and so on—are produced and who benefits from their production and circulation.

In contrast, an undergraduate education that advances shared problem-solving invites robust, critical discussions about value and about the ways in which value will be measured. As networks of problem-solvers take on local issues, they frame problems collaboratively, deciding together what issues matter and what solutions count as success. The process of shared problem-solving requires the network to deliberate about what problems are important, who needs to benefit from solutions, and what side effects are acceptable. We noted a discussion of value outlined in the ASU and Wake Forest final reports. We witnessed one first-hand in the MSI study. Students and staff in the programs in the MSI study, for example, were constantly pricing degrees in terms of dollars, effort, identities, and opportunities. The costs and potential value varied substantially. Some outcomes could not be given a price. For example, becoming a role model or learning the Cheyenne language was valued in terms of community development rather than tuition. The value of learning English often took into account students' needs to remain plugged in to communities that interacted in other languages. Costs created tension, forced individuals and institutions to balance what paid off and what they valued. Costs also led stakeholders on and off campus to rethink majors, programs, and transfer targets, but not their commitment to using education to address local problems.

This kind of thinking about value must, we believe, be intentional within programs that promote collaborative learning. Awareness of the alternatives notwithstanding, market value often seeps into and dominates considerations of what matters. Consider the fate of the triple bottom line, a framework that management consultant John Elkington introduced in the 1990s to measure the value produced by an enterprise in terms of social, environmental, and economic impact. In a 2018 *Harvard Business Review* article, Elkington reflected on and sought to "recall" the concept that he had coined 25 years earlier. He observed that this widely accepted framework had in practice been reduced to accounting for financial, environmental, and social performance in order to track the full financial cost of doing business. Missing, Elkington suggested, was a willingness to think about the preeminence of market value and the implications of unconsidered capitalism on the future of people in local communities and their ecological, social, and economic (as opposed to financial) well-being. The triple bottom line became an accounting tool for market value. As such, it did too little to deepen deliberations on what opportunities to pursue and what problems to solve.

Infusing entrepreneurship into undergraduate education can intentionally broaden and enrich the perspectives of students, staff, and faculty with respect to value creation. While entrepreneurial education often focuses on guiding students and faculty in bringing new products to market, taking an entrepreneurial approach to education also cultivates individual and institutional capacity to identify local opportunities and problems with stakeholders off campus and to leverage campus resources to find new ways to capitalize on opportunities and to solve problems. We see framing undergraduate education as entrepreneurial activity as a way to ask learners and teachers alike to expect to find new ways to solve problems and also to take part in ongoing critical dialogue about how to think about value and what value to create. Along the way, entrepreneurial undergraduate education positions learners and teachers as problem-solvers who build value with and for others.

Conclusion: Toward a Culturally Sustaining
Undergraduate Education

We see collaborative learning happening when groups of people—not only students and teachers but also staff members and members of local communities—take on shared endeavors that all participants find compelling. In exploring how collaborative learning finds expression in shared problem-solving, we have returned to what we learned at the MSIs and other institutions that are at work transforming undergraduate programs to make more space for every student to add value to ongoing local endeavors. These innovative, often entrepreneurial, programs map out a path that leads away from and around schooling in which teachers retain sole ownership of problems.

We are well aware that the path we propose leads to an alternative, even oppositional kind of education. At most campuses, most of the time students pursue their own individual problems as they seek an education that pays off for them: my grade, my major, my degree, my career. Not surprisingly, collaboration in undergraduate education is usually operationalized as cooperation and teamwork. Group projects are opportunities for individuals to show that they have acquired the skills of a team member and have contributed to a group project. Opportunities for collaborative learning such as those we have discussed are not what most students expect, desire, or aspire to when they matriculate.

A curriculum anchored in shared problem-solving challenges the conventional wisdom regarding the ends and the means of a college education. Programs designed around the framing and pursuit of shared problems require that students listen to others in order to find common needs, concerns, and interests. Courses, assignments, and extracurricular projects that take up shared problems draw problem-solvers into spirited dialogue through which they together and individually reflect on, question, and enlarge their understanding of the roots of problems. Success lies not so much in correct answers and carefully edited papers as in the development and implementation of solutions with and for those affected by problems. Shared problems make individual participants accountable to others in problem-solving and also with respect to sharing results. Problems take shape only as problem-solvers engage local contexts where problems emerge and forge reciprocal relationships with others who have a stake in the problem and its solution. Solving shared problems leads to the creation of new value as individuals put their understanding of the problem and the solutions that make sense to them out for review, assuming that a more complete solution is possible. In short, a curriculum that engages students with shared problems engages them in collaborative learning.

Over the past several decades, a growing number of colleges and universities have been exploring this kind of curriculum. These explorations start with rebranding undergraduate education as opportunity to become more skilled at tackling shared problems rather than courses to complete. The decision to reframe a college education seems to be a first step, but that step alone is not sufficient. Building a curriculum around solving shared problems is realized in a process of backwards design: in a sequence of required courses and assignments, students first describe their educational goals and then integrate those goals with the issues that their institution is addressing. Programs then require reflection on the problems through which students learn, the people who are affected by and working on those problems, and the kinds of solutions that have been tried or might be tried. This design thinking is tied to opportunities—often required—for students to learn how to learn and how to push projects forward and how to ensure that projects are sustainable.

In such a curriculum, students, staff, and faculty work with a pair of assumptions: others have something to contribute to the problem-solving process, and they themselves have an obligation to contribute to other's efforts at solving shared problems. Students start and finish their college experience as members of a series of problem-solving networks that are rooted in local communities. As participants in a network, students develop locally relevant knowledge and skills through linking their learning to local issues. Beyond the instrumental capacity to work on specific problems, their education comes with two other requirements. First, they are obligated to become able to learn with, for, and from others in the locales where important problems are anchored. Second, they are obligated to challenge received solutions and to look for new ways to use resources to create sustainable value.

The programs that we have explored in this chapter suggest a transformed role for institutions. Leaders at the MSIs—especially the Tribal Colleges and the Historically Black Colleges and Universities—explained that their institutions were either founded to play this role or had adopted the role so as to "serve" their students and their communities. For most American colleges and universities, this role requires transformational change. They will need to become "New American Universities," an identity ASU is pursuing to design socially relevant curricula and, as importantly, work out strategies to sustain community-engaged networks that empower and resource bottom-up local change and put new value to the test. They will continue to ask about return on investment, but they will need to frame that question carefully, asking not simply about financial returns but about how people and locales are impacted. In addition to opportunities to learn locally relevant knowledge and skills, their curricula provide formal and informal opportunities for students to learn how to develop ventures and then to implement them. They will need to wire into the undergraduate curriculum an expectation that students, staff, and faculty will move learning experiences and the fruits of learning off campus and into local communities.

In closing, we call attention to resonance between this kind of education—one anchored in real-world problem solving—and the culturally sustaining pedagogies being developed by Django Paris and others. In a 2012 *Education Researcher* essay, Paris sought to clarify and extend the asset pedagogy that Gloria Ladson-Billings formulated in her landmark 1995 article "Toward a Theory of Culturally Relevant Pedagogy." Paris offered "culturally sustaining pedagogy" as a way forward:

> The term culturally sustaining requires that our pedagogies be more than responsive of or relevant to the cultural experiences and practices of young people—it requires that they support young people in sustaining the cultural and linguistic competence of their communities while simultaneously offering access to dominant cultural competence. Culturally sustaining pedagogy, then, has as its explicit goal supporting multilingualism and multiculturalism in practice and perspective for students and teachers. That is, culturally sustaining pedagogy seeks to perpetuate and foster—to sustain—linguistic, literate, and cultural pluralism as part of the democratic project of schooling (95).

We understand an undergraduate education anchored in shared problem-solving to be culturally sustaining in these terms. Foremost, this type of education positions every learner as a full participant who brings social and cultural resources to college. Collaborative problem-solving invites students to contribute from their own repertoires of practice while learning and borrowing from those of others. At its best, the spirited dialogue that underlies shared problem-solving fosters "linguistic and cultural dexterity and plurality" in networks that value the resources that others bring (Paris 2009; 2011; 2012). Heritage practices provide ways of framing and solving problems, and they are grist for new mashups that emerge as diverse participants work together on collective endeavors.

Like culturally sustaining pedagogy, shared problem-solving, as we have come to understand it, has a critical edge. While all practices and identities are welcome in shared problem-solving, a shared endeavor and the capacity of the network to keep all participants contributing to the network are what sustain the community of practice. Identities and practices that exclude participants or deny them access to the resources they need to flourish work against shared problem-solving and against collaborative learning. Our time at the institutions in the MSI study led us to draw attention to two hedges against exclusivity and assimilation that seem to be baked into shared problem-solving. First, the 12 MSIs recognized and sustained the education of minoritized students by "mission and inclination." Diversity of experiences, identities, and practices enriches shared problem-solving, but it is the explicit valuing of the presence of minoritized students that makes problem-solving especially critical. Especially in programs at the Tribal Colleges and Universities and Historically Black Colleges and Universities but also those at the Hispanic-Serving Institutions and Asian American Native

American Pacific Islander Institutions, students of color and white students told us that they felt like the college was their college and that their stories and home communities were welcome. In turn, they felt empowered to use their own voices to ask their questions, ask for help, and help others. Staff and faculty confirmed that the programs were designed with those outcomes in mind. The goal, staff and faculty said again and again, was educating "whole people" and talking "frankly" about the ways in which undergraduate education often excluded minoritized identities. In this environment, shared problem-solving explicitly values contributions from students' home cultures and actively calls out exclusionary practices.

Second, the programs at the MSIs created opportunities for minoritized students to work on issues of importance to their own local communities. The Workforce Development Council Nursing Cohort program at North Seattle Community College was designed to work on two problems: providing access to nursing education to low-income, incumbent health care workers and diversifying the nursing labor force. Focused on the problem of attaining a nursing degree, a Latina in the program described her success by offering a convincing critique of the ways in which her immigrant status and poverty as well as racism in hiring practices and gender roles within her home influenced her educational opportunities. She punctuated her narrative with her surprise that "this time" she was succeeding. She went on to explain what contributed to her success: in required meetings with program mentors and instructors, together they framed her challenges and possible resources; in further dialogue with her peers, they began to innovate, to coop childcare and to decide which small groups would best support her success. This is one of numerous examples where a diverse network engaged in collaborative learning made space to document barriers and exclusion and then to crowd source workarounds.

To be sure, many of the workarounds left exclusionary structures in place. Yet, at the same time, collaborative innovations redefined institutional narratives about student success and paved the way for other students to follow. The students were, often by their own admission, unlikely "role models." At a minimum, these workarounds forced the institution to recognize alternative routes to success. At best, they were institutionalized. At San Diego City College, unlikely students got jobs as peer mentors; at the College of Menominee Nation, American Indian students traveled from the Reservation to national conferences and founded chapters of national organizations at their Tribal College. Refusing to relinquish the heritages or the educational goals of their students, these institutions empowered faculty to teach differently and pressured program and institutional cultures to problematize traditional education.

Anchoring the undergraduate curriculum in shared problem-solving has the potential to open American higher education to the needs and resources of the increasingly diverse students who enroll and the increasingly diverse communities that make up our nation. This path to collaborative learning is a route to an undergraduate education that meets the needs of our diverse democracy, one that sustains our diverse cultures while holding space for intercultural collaborations that solve local problems. It is a path that institutions that continue to stick to mainstream practices at PWIs may find unachievable.

Undergraduate Education for Twenty-First-Century America

Beyond Predominantly White Undergraduate Education

We began this project by following up on a theme that overlapped the twelve case studies in the Minority-Serving Institutions (MSI) Models study (Conrad and Gasman 2015). Programs at the MSIs were establishing and sustaining networks of students, staff, and faculty to engage in collaborative learning aimed at addressing challenges and opportunities facing minoritized students and their communities. These programs had collected evidence that showed increased access, persistence, and learning for minoritized students. We decided to write a book about practices that made these programs work rather than a book about MSIs or about the impact of race and racism on undergraduate education. Drawing on what we learned at the MSIs, we then went on to identify "pockets of innovation" at Predominantly White Institutions (PWIs) that were incorporating shared problem-solving into the undergraduate experience. Reading across these MSIs and PWIs, we wrote the first draft of this book focused on programs and practices that would elevate the place of collaborative learning in undergraduate education and, in so doing, promote the success of all undergraduates in American colleges and universities.

In writing this book, we became increasingly aware of a contradiction in our purpose that has in many ways framed our practices as teachers, researchers, and administrators in higher education. To illustrate, as a white teacher and staff member, I (Todd) spent most of my career trying to improve the PWIs at which I worked, and my identities routinely gave me access to leadership positions. A decade of teaching in the rust belt at Cleveland State University and the University of Wisconsin–Milwaukee (1993–2003) challenged my basic assumptions about making undergraduate education better. I became increasingly aware that these PWIs in segregated cities had been designed to fail many of the students who were trying to make it through my writing classes. I began intentionally reworking a curriculum that had asked my students to assimilate to a culture that was hostile to their home identities and their success in college.

This contradiction intensified for me when I moved to an innovative predominantly white community college in suburban Seattle. As an institution, Cascadia Community College was committed to a transparent curriculum, co-teaching, group work, and equity. Yet, as a teacher and administrator, I observed many students picking up credentials but often being confused by my teaching practices that asked them to learn from one another and reflect critically on what their education was for. More troubling were the equity gaps that my institution labored to recognize and close. The few minoritized students who made it to my classrooms and offices often seemed alienated and frustrated by the hidden curriculum at my transfer-oriented community college. Minoritized staff and faculty colleagues often described being alienated and exhausted. I understood that American higher education often had these impacts, yet I kept looking for ways to improve my PWI and support its mission. I stepped away from teaching to pick up a doctorate in higher education and joined the MSI Models study. I then returned to Cascadia as a dean and tried to implement what I was learning about educating minoritized students.

I (Clif) became aware of this contradiction beginning several decades ago as I had visited scores of PWIs and MSIs—the latter as an expert witness for the US Department of Justice in higher education desegregation cases in nine states. In these cases, I heard again and again at Historically Black Colleges and Universities (HBCUs) how unwelcome many minority students felt at PWIs and that their learning experiences at these institutions were not often linked to the challenges facing the communities from which they came. As we completed the MSI study, I began to appreciate the problem. I have spent much of my career exploring practices aimed at transforming mainstream higher education in ways that would not only help to eradicate racist policies and practices but would also enrich the learning experiences of all students. In my own teaching, I began putting into practice what I was learning from MSIs and revisioning many of my teaching practices—such as co-teaching with students. I have long been a professor at PWIs that have struggled in many ways to welcome and support minoritized students with respect to their learning and their persistence in college.

In writing this book, the contradiction between our desire to elaborate on the educational practices that we had learned about at the MSIs and our desire to describe practices that could improve American higher education came to center stage as we looked at interview transcripts and program documents in the MSI Models Study database. As we listened to voices represented in the database, we heard again and again a commitment to a different approach to undergraduate education. Our work shifted from parsing educational practices to listening to how individuals described their participation in programs. As we pieced together this "different approach" to undergraduate education at MSIs, we started calling it "collaborative learning." Most students, staff, and faculty had adopted a script for student success in college that runs counter to the script used at most colleges and universities. As we documented practices that promote collaborative learning at the MSIs and at PWIs, we realized that we needed to map out a different approach.

In finishing this book, we draw attention to what we make of this difference in scripts. We shift our focus from practices and programs and even colleges and universities to the institution of American higher education. The script for collaborative learning that we outline in the book was articulated and shaped by programs at MSIs for the most part—colleges and universities that have a complex relationship to American higher education. Assessing the place of Hispanic-Serving Institutions (HSIs) in American education, Gina Garcia (2019) observed that American higher education is embedded in a society that has assigned value to individuals, groups, and organizations based on ideas about race. Colleges and universities are racialized not by the inherent characteristics and capabilities of students but through a social process that assigns power and privilege to individuals, groups, and organizations based on racial categories.

Notwithstanding progress on desegregation in higher education along with efforts to increase diversity and a growing recognition of racism on campus. American undergraduate education has been primarily designed for individuals from predominantly white communities and high schools—with most students having had limited contact with communities of color (Brunsma, Brown, and Placier 2013). This educational script was written by and for PWIs. American undergraduate education authorizes individuals as graduates and confers on them the status and competitive advantage that comes with that role (Meyer et al. 2007), and, in turn, student success and failure are explained in large measure by the extent to which individual students are integrated into a developmental process designed for college-ready white individuals (Rendón, Jalomo, and Nora 2000; Tierney 1992). Colleges and universities are ranked, Garcia argues, based on how closely their practices—selecting a student body, establishing a curriculum, and assessing student success—are aligned with cultivating white graduates. Typically located close to communities of color, MSIs "serve" by mission or by fact students who are identified as not white or who do not wish to identify as white. As Garcia observes, their places and purposes mark MSIs as colleges and universities that are less valued within a social institution in which student success means assimilation into predominantly white identities and practices.

While the status quo script for American higher education was developed by and for PWIs, as Garcia notes and we observed, MSIs are spaces where that script is being rewritten. Drawing on the method of counter-storytelling (Solórzano and Yosso 2002), Garcia describes ways in which HSIs both "provide great value to the students they serve and the system as a whole" and also "maintain the racial order of the system" (26). While the stories we heard in the MSI study were as unique as the study participants, across them a shared awareness of and resistance to the status quo emerged as students and staff at the MSIs explained the kind of undergraduate education they were seeking. They came to their colleges looking for programs that welcome students and their identities rather than programs that promoted assimilation to the social and academic communities that many had experienced at PWIs. Moreover, they came to these programs to design and enact an education that they could use to improve their own lives and the minoritized communities from which many came and, in so doing, challenge American racism and American education. As narrators in their own stories, they refused not to tell their own stories, and they explained to predominantly white researchers—often though not always with patience and respectfulness—the impact of racism and the need for educated people with their experiences and the need for educational institutions designed to value their experiences and goals.

Like many white educators, we began this project exploring and documenting educational practices that improve opportunities to learn for all students—our focus on underrepresented minorities notwithstanding. We did not acknowledge up front that most programs and practices nested within PWIs and also MSIs fail to reckon sufficiently with the ways in which they reproduce an education that pegs success to whiteness. The stories of students, staff, and faculty at the MSIs in the study called out that question. They welcomed us on their campuses to talk about improving American undergraduate education and then outlined for us the institutional blueprints and building blocks along with the conflicting interests and adaptations they had to negotiate in order to improve the education of minoritized students. Many people we spoke with at the MSIs described having to hack American higher education, a social institution that normalizes whiteness. They spoke openly about how traditional undergraduate programs were built to educate college-ready students from college-preparatory high schools. They emphasized the importance of non-white spaces where students could participate without assimilating and where their funds of knowledge were valued and valuable. They made no bones about how underresourced and marginalized these spaces were within American undergraduate education. Administrators at MSIs emphasized the creative ways they successfully pursued funding for these spaces. Students at MSIs found them and made them home.

The participants in the MSI Models study gave us a glimpse at undergraduate education designed for minoritized students, a glimpse of a counter-story. These programs were building alternate social spaces in which whiteness is not predominant and does not dominate. They were writing an educational script that assumes that minority students and staff matter rather than one that allows that minority students and staff are welcome to participate. Through their programs and practices, the MSIs had defined student success as becoming able to join with others in solving shared problems, including the problem of getting an education in an American college or university without becoming white. The programs at the MSIs consistently subordinated predominantly white, mainstream measures of success—such as persistence, grades, graduation, and even access—to the health of networks and the progress of networks in solving shared problems. It is not that predominantly white measures of success did not matter. Students wanted degrees and A's, and their teachers wanted them to earn degrees and A's. Rather, those benchmarks were relocated on a different developmental trajectory. Degrees were valuable to the extent that having a degree brought value to the lives of minoritized students in their own communities. One Tribal College administrator described with exasperation well-meaning mainstream strategies for solving the problem of remedial education by ensuring all college students were college ready before they started college. For her and her colleagues, learning and education that mattered had to "matter" on a reservation with limited educational resources and little reason to trust mainstream education in America. They had little interest in selecting students based on their being already prepared to enter a predominantly white social institution.

Put simply, the MSIs scaffolded collaborative learning and, in so doing, created space within American higher education for antiracist work as described by Gooden, Davis, Spikes, Hall, and Lee (2018) and Asao Inoue (2015). Race was always out in the open. Students, staff, and faculty knew that race did not name inherent characteristics or abilities and, at the same time, that race had already classified individuals and groups and spaces and also predetermined access to resources and status in American society. The MSIs emphasized throughout the undergraduate experience—from courses to outside-of-class experiences—that Native American, Black, Hispanic, and Alaskan Native, Asian American, and Pacific Islander students' identities were valuable. Opportunities to reflect on their identities and receive feedback on their participation were incorporated across the curriculum, and staff and faculty were reimagining the ways that classes, courses, and programs could engage participants more deeply in solving local problems that were relevant to the lives of students. Participation itself was antiracist action, the ongoing identification and dismantling of barriers often facing minoritized students in a predominantly white social institution.

Programs at the MSIs were not simply adding "group work" to the American undergraduate curriculum. They were promoting collaborative learning: learning with, from, and for others. They were writing and running an institutional script that positioned undergraduate education not as the cultivation of predominantly white capabilities and mindsets but as participation in shared problem-solving in local endeavors by people who were learning to make local communities thrive. The script called for what Raymond Williams (1989) called "adult education": education designed to be part of the process of social change rather than a contribution to social change. We reworked our analysis to piece together pathways to this different approach to undergraduate education.

And then 2020 happened. As we neared completion of this manuscript, we watched the COVID-19 pandemic lay bare social inequalities and shut down campuses across the country. We read statistics on the disparate impact of the virus on communities of color; we watched a police officer kneel on the neck of George Floyd; we observed faculty trying to engage students through learning management systems and video conference platforms that the faculty themselves were learning while they managed chaotic home lives, protested, and counter-protested. We wondered about the value of a book on programs and practices that promote collaborative learning rather than one on antiracist education or on teaching during a period of social disruption. We came to think of this book as a lever for transformation. Collaborative learning is an overarching template and a set of practices that are part of a continual process of re-setting norms and values, rethinking identities and roles, communicating about participation, and deciding what problems are worth solving. An education anchored in collaborative learning holds open questions about how privilege and power are allocated and the ways in which mainstream educational practices reproduce inequity; at the same time it rewrites the expectations that students, staff, and faculty have for how they will participate in educational programs and the expected outcomes of those programs.

Our exploration of MSI practices led us to believe that undergraduate education structured as collaborative learning has the potential to serve the United States as our nation finds its way in the twenty-first century. Undergraduate education grounded in collaborative learning has the potential to prepare graduates to participate more fully in a global democracy that is negotiating widening social inequalities, political polarization, and formidable environmental challenges. An education anchored in collaborative learning obligates every participant to value every other participant and expands the definition of educational success to include progress in solving shared problems as well as in degrees earned, jobs secured, and communities engaged.

The educational programs and practices we have highlighted in this book emerged in contexts that were intentionally rewriting the script for predominantly white undergraduate education. The practice of collaborative learning is critical and reflective and always responsive to who is in the network and where the network is situated. Rather than another framework designed to work at a PWI, collaborative learning is an educational process that is guided by the shared problems that participants agree to take up, and the choice of shared problems is always up for review. The practices that we explore here take students, staff, and teachers below the surface of undergraduate education. Measures of success shift from who earned what degree with what grades to what problems were framed, what solutions were developed, and how did networks move the process of problem-solving forward. Collaborative learning engages all participants in critical reflection on relationships, influence, power, and value.

Collaborative learning gives newbies a seat at the table, asks experts to depend on newbies. The process of collaborative learning expects and works through resistance and asks participants to own their resistances.

The educational practices we explore in this book are flexible and entrepreneurial, and we cannot help but wonder how collaborative learners might have managed the pivot to emergency remote instruction that began in the spring of 2020. Faculty struggled to learn and implement technologies for reproducing classrooms online while their worlds were turned upside down, and students wrestled to access technology and find time and motivation in the midst of distraction and crisis. Everyone struggled with bandwidth and, for the most part, everyone waited for the pivot to remote instruction to end. While strategies for collaboration in online classes are well established and successful, forging or maintaining a commitment to collaboration felt for many like too much.

By the spring of 2021, after a year of remote emergency instruction, with Clif teaching classes and Todd providing instructional support for faculty, we began talking about how the pivot might have been managed by students, staff, and faculty already engaged in collaborative learning. Collaborative learners view courses and programs as sandboxes in which to learn how to be interdependent and how to flourish together as they tackle shared problems. Staff and faculty, with institutional support, make it their business to know where students come from, and they structure opportunities to learn so that students can draw on their social and cultural identities and experiences. Might colleges and universities structure emergency instruction so that students can participate from home or quarantine as an extension of current practice, disruptive though it must be? Moreover, might students, staff, and faculty engaged in collaborative learning be more prepared for the kind of disruption that we have experienced? These participants expect to shift among roles. They depend on others to pursue a shared endeavor while they themselves are dependable. They share the expectation that everyone—old hands and novices—is working on a wicked problem and will contribute to a more complete response across multiple attempts. Processes for providing feedback and feedforward are in place and time has already been allocated for them. Since collaborative learners expect to innovate so as to solve local problems, might they be more open to the hacks that kept undergraduate education going in a pandemic? Might they be better positioned to carry forward temporary innovations into whatever happens next? We wonder.

We see great promise in each of the programs and practices that we explored. But are different programs and practices enough to disrupt the myth that individual learning and achievement is enough? We wonder. We see no reason to believe that better-educated individual learners who know how to cooperate and even have thought critically about a tradition of exclusionary education will be prepared to flourish and contribute in our rapidly changing and diverse nation and world. As do advocates of Universal Design and antiracist education, we point to the need for a "different approach." Although they rarely mentioned reform initiatives like Universal Design or antiracism or collaborative learning, the MSIs were trying to become educational spaces that minimized barriers to learning and, in so doing, enhanced the learning of every student. Taking diversity in experience, identity, interests, and ability as a given, they were establishing equitable and flexible educational programs that empowered every student to participate and learn. The twelve

MSIs—Tribal Colleges seemed the most intentional—were designing programs for all of the students they served, whether or not others viewed those students as college ready.

An education anchored in collaborative learning has the potential to disrupt the widely shared commitment to credentialing individual learners and, in so doing, to establish educational spaces in which all students now coming to American colleges and universities can find opportunities to try out and advance the identities and capacities at use in communities of practice that are engaged in responding to shared problems. This kind of undergraduate education has the potential to provide a diverse democracy and world with graduates who have practiced bridging social inequalities and political divisions and solving shared challenges including social inequalities, political divisions, and compromised local and global ecosystems. We invite our colleges and universities to learn *with* and *from* institutions—including their programs and practices—that successfully serve minoritized students by establishing networks of learners that minimize barriers to learning, maximize the learning of all participants, and ask every participant to learn *for* others.

REFERENCES

Argyris, Chris. 1999. *On Organizational Learning*. Malden, MA: Blackwell.

Arizona State University. 2012. "Arizona State University as a Kauffman Campus, 2007–2011." Kansas City, MO: Ewing Marion Kauffman Foundation. https://www.kauffman.org/-/media/kauffman_org /research-reports-and-covers/2013/08/kci_asu.pdf?la=en.

Association of American Colleges and Universities. 2007. "College Learning for the New Global Century: A Report from the National Leadership Council for Liberal Education & America's Promise." 0-9779-2104-2. Washington, DC: Association of American Colleges and Universities. http://www.aacu.org/leap/documents/GlobalCentury_final.pdf.

Astin, Alexander W. 1987. "Competition or Cooperation? Teaching Teamwork as a Basic Skill." *Change* 19 (5): 12–19.

———. 1993. *What Matters in College? Four Critical Years Revisited*. San Francisco: Jossey-Bass.

Attinasi, Louis C. 1989. "Getting In: Mexican Americans' Perceptions of University Attendance and the Implications for Freshman Year Persistence." *Journal of Higher Education* 60 (3): 247–77.

Auchincloss, Lisa Corwin, Sandra L. Laursen, Janet L. Branchaw, Kevin Eagan, Mark Graham, David I. Hanauer, Gwendolyn Lawrie, et al. 2014. "Assessment of Course-Based Undergraduate Research Experiences: A Meeting Report." *CBE—Life Sciences Education* 13 (1): 29–40.

Autor, David H. 2014. "Skills, Education, and the Rise of Earnings Inequality among the 'other 99 Percent.'" *Science* 344 (6186): 843–51.

Bailey, Thomas R., Shanna Smith Jaggars, and Davis Jenkins. 2015. *Redesigning America's Community Colleges: A Clearer Path to Student Success*. Cambridge, MA: Harvard University Press.

Bain, Ken. 2004. *What the Best College Teachers Do*. Cambridge, MA: Harvard University Press.

Bangera, Gita, and Sara E. Brownell. 2014. "Course-Based Undergraduate Research Experiences Can Make Scientific Research More Inclusive." *CBE—Life Sciences Education* 13 (4): 602–6.

Barber, Benjamin R. 1992. *An Aristocracy of Everyone: The Politics of Education and the Future of Democracy*. New York: Ballantine Books.

Barkley, Elizabeth F., Claire Howell Major, and K. Patricia Cross. 2014. *Collaborative Learning Techniques: A Handbook for College Faculty*. 2nd ed. The Jossey-Bass Higher and Adult Education Series. San Francisco: Jossey-Bass.

Barr, Robert B., and John Tagg. 1995. "From Teaching to Learning—A New Paradigm for Undergraduate Education. (Cover Story)." *Change* 27 (6): 13–25.

Baum, Sandy, Jennifer Ma, and Kathleen Payea. 2013. "Education Pays 2013: The Benefits of Higher Education for Individuals and Society." The College Board. http://trends.collegeboard.org/sites/default/files /education-pays-2013-full-report.pdf.

Bean, John C. 2011. *Engaging Ideas: The Professor's Guide to Integrating Writing, Critical Thinking, and Active Learning in the Classroom*. 2nd ed. San Francisco: Jossey-Bass.

Bennett, Randy Elliot. 2011. "Formative Assessment: A Critical Review." *Assessment in Education: Principles, Policy & Practice* 18 (1): 5–25.

Bergom, Inger, Mary C. Wright, Marie Kendall Brown, and Michael Brooks. 2011. "Promoting College Student Development through Collaborative Learning: A Case Study of Hevruta." *About Campus*, February 2011.

Bertman, Stephen. 2010. *The Genesis of Science: The Story of Greek Imagination*. Amherst, NY: Prometheus Books.

Blum, Susan D. 2016. *"I Love Learning, I Hate School": An Anthropology of College*. Ithaca, NY: Cornell University Press.

Bonilla-Silva, Eduardo. 2018. *Racism without Racists: Color-Blind Racism and the Persistence of Racial Inequality in America*. 5th ed. Lanham, MD: Rowman & Littlefield.

Boud, David, and Elizabeth Molloy. 2013. "Rethinking Models of Feedback for Learning: The Challenge of Design." *Assessment & Evaluation in Higher Education* 38 (6): 698–712.

Boyer Commission on Educating Undergraduates in the Research
University. 1998. "Reinventing Undergraduate Education: A
Blueprint for America's Research Universities." Stoney Brook: State
University of New York, Stoney Brook. http://eric.ed.gov/?id
=ED424840.

Boyer, Ernest L. 1990. "Scholarship Reconsidered." New York: Carnegie
Foundation for the Advancement of Teaching.

———. 1996. "The Scholarship of Engagement." *Bulletin of the American
Academy of Arts and Sciences* 49 (7): 18–33.

Bransford, John, A. L. Brown, and R. R. Cocking. 2000. *How People Learn:
Brain, Mind, Experience, and School.* Washington, DC: National
Academies Press.

Braxton, John M., Mardy T. Eimers, and Alan E. Bayer. 1996. "The
Implications of Teaching Norms for the Improvement of Undergraduate Education." *Journal of Higher Education* 67 (December): 603–25.

Bringle, Robert G., and Julie A. Hatcher. 2009. "Innovative Practices in
Service-Learning and Curricular Engagement." *New Directions for
Higher Education* 147: 37–46.

Bruffee, Kenneth A. 1999. *Collaborative Learning: Higher Education,
Interdependence, and the Authority of Knowledge.* 2nd ed. Baltimore,
MD: Johns Hopkins University Press.

Bruner, Jerome Seymour. 1996. *The Culture of Education.* Cambridge, MA:
Harvard University Press.

Brunsma, David L., Eric S. Brown, and Peggy Placier. 2013. "Teaching
Race at Historically White Colleges and Universities: Identifying
and Dismantling the Walls of Whiteness." *Critical Sociology* 39 (5):
717–38.

Buck, Laura B., Stacey Lowery Bretz, and Marcy H. Towns. 2008.
"Characterizing the Level of Inquiry in the Undergraduate Laboratory." *Journal of College Science Teaching* 38: 52–58.

Burgstahler, Sheryl E. 2015. "Universal Design in Higher Education."
In *Universal Design in Higher Education: From Principles to Practices*,
edited by Sheryl E. Burgstahler, 3–28. Cambridge, MA: Harvard
Education Press.

Butin, Dan W. 2012. "When Engagement Is Not Enough: Building the
next Generation of the Engaged Campus." In *The Engaged Campus:
Certificates, Minors and Majors as the New Community Engagement*,
edited by Dan W. Butin and Scott Seider, 1–11. New York: Palgrave
Macmillan.

Carless, David, Diane Salter, Min Yang, and Joy Lam. 2011. "Developing Sustainable Feedback Practices." *Studies in Higher Education* 36 (4): 395–407.

Carnevale, Anthony P., Nicole Smith, and Jeff Strohl. 2010. "Help Wanted: Projections of Jobs and Education Requirements through 2018." Washington, DC: Georgetown University Center on Education and the Workforce. https://georgetown.app.box.com/s/ursjbxaym 2np1v8mgrv7.

Carpenter, Rowena. 2015. "University Studies Assessment Report, 2014–2015." Portland, OR: Portland State University. https://www .pdx.edu/unst/sites/www.pdx.edu.unst/files/14-15%20UNST%20 Annual%20Assessment%20Report.pdf.

CAST. 2018. "Universal Design for Learning Guidelines, Version 2.2." Graphic organizer. http://udlguidelines.cast.org/.

Castellanos, Jeanett, and Alberta M. Gloria. 2007. "Research Considerations and Theoretical Application for Best Practices in Higher Education." *Journal of Hispanic Higher Education* 6 (4): 378–96.

Center for Universal Design. 1997. "The Principles of Universal Design, Version 2.0." Raleigh: North Carolina State University. http://www .ncsu.edu/ncsu/design/cud/about_ud/udprinciplestext.htm.

Chickering, Arthur W., and Zelda F. Gamson. 1987. "Seven Principles for Good Practice in Undergraduate Education." *AAHE Bulletin*, March 1987.

Chickering, Arthur W., and Linda Reisser. 1993. *Education and Identity.* San Francisco: Jossey-Bass.

Chua, Amy. 2018. *Political Tribes: Group Instinct and the Fate of Nations.* New York: Penguin Books.

Clark, Burton R. 1998. *Creating Entrepreneurial Universities: Organizational Pathways of Transformation.* New York: Pergamon.

Cohen, Arthur M., and Carrie B. Kisker. 2010. *The Shaping of American Higher Education: Emergence and Growth of the Contemporary System.* 2nd ed. San Francisco: Jossey-Bass.

Commission on the Future of Undergraduate Education. 2017. "The Future of Undergraduate Education: The Future of America." Final Report and Recommendations. Cambridge, MA: American Academy of Arts & Sciences. https://www.amacad.org/sites/default/files /publication/downloads/Future-of-Undergraduate-Education.pdf.

Condliffe, Barbara, and Associates. 2017. "Project-Based Learning: A Literature Review." New York: MDRC. https://files.eric.ed.gov /fulltext/ED578933.pdf.

Conrad, Clifton F., and Laura Dunek. 2020. *Cultivating Inquiry-Driven Learners: A College Education for the 21st Century*. 2nd ed. Baltimore, MD: Johns Hopkins University Press.

Conrad, Clifton F., and Marybeth Gasman. 2015. *Educating a Diverse Nation: Lessons from Minority-Serving Institutions*. Cambridge, MA: Harvard University Press.

Cowan, John. 2010. "Developing the Ability for Making Evaluative Judgements." *Teaching in Higher Education* 15 (3): 323–34.

Cross, Nigel. 2011. *Design Thinking: Understanding How Designers Think and Work*. New York: Oxford University Press.

Davis, James R. 1995. *Interdisciplinary Courses and Team Teaching: New Arrangements for Learning*. Phoenix, AZ: Ace/Oryx.

Dawson, Phillip, Michael Henderson, Paige Mahoney, Michael Phillips, Tracii Ryan, David Boud, and Elizabeth Molloy. 2019. "What Makes for Effective Feedback: Staff and Student Perspectives." *Assessment & Evaluation in Higher Education* 44 (1): 25–36.

Deeley, Susan J., and Catherine Bovill. 2017. "Staff Student Partnership in Assessment: Enhancing Assessment Literacy through Democratic Practices." *Assessment & Evaluation in Higher Education* 42 (3): 463–77.

Dees, J. Gregory. 2001. "The Meaning of 'Social Entrepreneurship.'" Durham, NC: Center for the Advancement of Social Entrepreneurship, Duke University. https://centers.fuqua.duke.edu/case/wp -content/uploads/sites/7/2015/03/Article_Dees_Meaningof SocialEntrepreneurship_2001.pdf.

Dewey, John. 1938. *Experience and Education*. New York: Macmillan.

Dolan, Erin L. 2017. "Course-Based Undergraduate Research Experiences: Current Knowledge and Future Directions." Washington, DC: Board on Science Education, National Academies of Sciences, Engineering, and Medicine. https://sites.nationalacademies.org/cs /groups/dbassesite/documents/webpage/dbasse_177288.pdf.

Dunn, Lee, and Michelle Wallace. 2008. "Intercultural Communities of Practice." In *Teaching in Transnational Higher Education: Enhancing Learning for Offshore International Students*, edited by Lee Dunn and Michelle Wallace, 249–60. New York: Routledge.

Eagan, M. Kevin, Jr., Sylvia Hurtado, Mitchell J. Chang, Gina Ann Garcia, Felisha A. Herrera, and Juan C. Garibay. 2013. "Making a Difference in Science Education: The Impact of Undergraduate Research Programs." *American Educational Research Journal* 50 (4): 683–713.

Edmondson, Amy C. 2012. *Teaming: How Organizations Learn, Innovate, and Compete in the Knowledge Economy.* San Francisco: Jossey-Bass.

Eisen, Mary-Jane. 2000. "The Many Faces of Team Teaching and Learning: An Overview." *New Directions for Adult & Continuing Education,* no. 87: 5–14.

Elkington, John. 2018. "25 Years Ago I Coined the Phrase 'Triple Bottom Line.' Here's Why It's Time to Rethink It." *Harvard Business Review Digital Articles,* June, 2–5.

Engeström, Yrjö. 2008. *From Teams to Knots: Activity-Theoretical Studies of Collaboration and Learning at Work.* New York: Cambridge University Press.

Espinosa, Lorelle L., Jonathan M. Turk, Morgan Taylor, and Hollie M. Chessman. 2019. "Race and Ethnicity in Higher Education: A Status Report." Washington, DC: American Council on Education. https://www.acenet.edu/Research-Insights/Pages/Race-and-Ethnicity-in-Higher-Education.aspx.

Evans, Carol. 2013. "Making Sense of Assessment Feedback in Higher Education." *Review of Educational Research* 83 (1): 70–120.

Ewing Marion Kauffman Foundation. 2013. "Entrepreneurship Education Comes of Age on Campus: The Challenges and Rewards of Bringing Entrepreneurship to Higher Education." Kansas City, MO: Ewing Marion Kauffman Foundation. https://www.kauffman.org/-/media/kauffman_org/research-reports-and-covers/2013/08/eshipedcomesofage_report.pdf.

Eyler, Janet, and Dwight E. Giles. 1999. *Where's the Learning in Service-Learning? Where Is the Learning in Service-Learning?* San Francisco: Jossey-Bass.

Fitzpatrick, Erika. 2007. "Innovation America: A Final Report." Washington, DC: National Governors Association. http://www.nga.org/files/live/sites/NGA/files/pdf/0707INNOVATIONFINAL.PDF.

Flynn, Erin. 2015. "From Capstones to Strategic Partnerships: The Evolution of Portland State University's Community Engagement and Partnership Agenda." *Metropolitan Universities* 26 (3): 159–70.

Friedman, Thomas L. 2011. "Global Challenges Facing America and the Role of Education in U.S. Competitiveness." Speech presented at the

National Governors Association Annual Meeting, Salt Lake City, UT, July 17. https://www.c-span.org/video/?300480-1/national-governors -association-annual-meeting-thomas-friedman-remarks.

Frost, Gail, and Maureen Connolly. 2015. "The Road Less Travelled? Pathways from Passivity to Agency in Student Learning." *Collected Essays on Learning & Teaching* 8 (January): 47–54.

Gallup Inc. 2014. "Great Jobs, Great Lives: The 2014 Gallup-Purdue Index Report." Washington, DC: Gallup Inc. https://www.gallup.com/services /176768/2014-gallup-purdue-index-report.aspx.

Garcia, Gina Ann. 2019. *Becoming Hispanic-Serving Institutions: Opportunities for Colleges and Universities*. Reforming Higher Education: Innovation and the Public Good. Baltimore, MD: Johns Hopkins University Press.

Gasman, Marybeth, Thai-Huy Nguyen, Clifton F. Conrad, Todd C. Lundberg, and Felecia Commodore. 2017. "Black Male Success in STEM: A Case Study of Morehouse College." *Journal of Diversity in Higher Education* 10 (2): 181–200.

Gatewood, Elizabeth, William F. Conner, and Page West. 2012. "Changing a Campus Culture: The Role of the Kauffman Campus Initiative in Promoting Entrepreneurship at Wake Forest University." Kansas City, MO: Ewing Marion Kauffman Foundation. https://www.kauffman .org/-/media/kauffman_org/research-reports-and-covers/2013/08 /kci_wakeforest.pdf?la=en.

Gee, James Paul. 2003. *What Video Games Have to Teach Us about Learning and Literacy*. 1st ed. New York: Palgrave Macmillan.

Gibbons, Michael, Camille Limoges, Helga Nowotny, Simon Schwartzman, Peter Scott, and Martin Trow. 1994. *The New Production of Knowledge: The Dynamics of Science and Research in Contemporary Societies*. Thousand Oaks, CA: SAGE Publications.

Gilyard, Keith. 1991. *Voices of the Self: A Study of Language Competence*. Detroit, MI: Wayne State University Press.

Gloria, Alberta M., and Jeanett Castellanos. 2003. "Latino/a and African American Students at Predominantly White Institutions: A Psychosociocultural Perspective of Educational Interactions and Academic Persistence." In *The Majority in the Minority: Retaining Latina/o Faculty, Administrators, and Students*, edited by Jeanett Castellanos and L. Jones, 71–92. Sterling, VA: Stylus.

Gloria, Alberta M., and Sharon E. Robinson-Kurpius. 1996. "The Validation of the Cultural Congruity Scale and the University

Environment Scale with Chicano/a Students." *Hispanic Journal of Behavioral Sciences* 18 (January): 533–49.

Goode, Christopher, Melissa Demetrikopoulos, Shari Britner, Laura Carruth, Brian Williams, John Pecore, Robert DeHaan, and Kyle Frantz. 2018. "Collaborative vs. Apprenticed Undergraduate Research Experiences." *Understanding Interventions Journal* 9 (1). https://www.understandinginterventionsjournal.org/article/3526-collaborative-vs-apprenticed-undergraduate-research-experiences.

Gooden, Mark A., Bradley Davis, Daniel Spikes, Dottie Hall, and Linda Lee. 2018. "Leaders Changing How They Act by Changing How They Think: Applying Principles of an Anti-Racist Principal Preparation Program." *Teachers College Record* 120 (14): 1–26.

Goodsell, Anne S., Michelle Maher, Vincent Tinto, Barbara Leigh Smith, and Jean MacGregor. 1992. *Collaborative Learning: A Sourcebook for Higher Education.* University Park, PA: National Center on Postsecondary Teaching, Learning, and Assessment.

Grioux, Henry A. 2002. "Neoliberalism, Corporate Culture, and the Promise of Higher Education: The University as a Democratic Public Sphere." *Harvard Educational Review* 72 (4): 425–63.

Grubb, W. Norton, and Marvin Lazerson. 2005. "The Education Gospel and the Role of Vocationalism in American Education." *American Journal of Education* 111 (3): 297–319.

Guiffrida, Douglas A. 2006. "Toward a Cultural Advancement of Tinto's Theory." *Review of Higher Education* 29 (4): 451–72.

Guillory, Justin P., and Kelly Ward. 2008. "Tribal Colleges and Universities: Identity, Invisibility, and Current Issues." In *Understanding Minority-Serving Institutions*, edited by Marybeth Gasman, Benjamin Baez, and Caroline Sotello Viernes Turner, 91–110. Albany: State University of New York Press.

Hanstedt, Paul. 2018. *Creating Wicked Students: Designing Courses for a Complex World.* Sterling, VA: Stylus.

Harris, Candace, and Anne N. C. Harvey. 2000. "Team Teaching in Adult Higher Education Classrooms: Toward Collaborative Knowledge Construction." *New Directions for Adult & Continuing Education*, no. 87: 25–32.

Harris, Joseph. 1989. "The Idea of Community in the Study of Writing." *College Composition & Communication* 40 (February): 11–22.

Haswell, Richard. 2006. "The Complexities of Responding to Student Writing; Or, Looking for Shortcuts via the Road of Excess." *Across*

the Disciplines 3 (November). https://wac.colostate.edu/docs/atd
/articles/haswell2006.pdf.

Hattie, John, and Helen Timperley. 2007. "The Power of Feedback."
Review of Educational Research 77 (1): 81–112.

Hawe, Eleanor, and Helen Dixon. 2017. "Assessment for Learning: A
Catalyst for Student Self-Regulation." *Assessment & Evaluation in
Higher Education* 42 (8): 1181–92.

Hoffer, Eric. 1951. *The True Believer: Thoughts on the Nature of Mass
Movements.* New York: Harper & Row.

Hoy, Ariane, Mathew Johnson, and Robert Hackett. 2012. "Disciplining
Higher Education for Democratic Community Engagement." In *The
Engaged Campus: Certificates, Minors and Majors as the New Commu-
nity Engagement,* edited by Dan W. Butin and Scott Seider, 177–86.
New York: Palgrave Macmillan.

Hunter, Anne-Barrie, Timothy J. Weston, Sandra L. Laursen, and Heather
Thiry. 2009. "Evaluating Student Gains from Undergraduate Research
in the Sciences." *Council on Undergraduate Research Quarterly* 29 (3):
15–19.

Hurtado, Sylvia, and Deborah Faye Carter. 1997. "Effects of College
Transition and Perceptions of the Campus Racial Climate on Latino
Students' Sense of Belonging." *Sociology of Education* 70 (4): 324–45.

Inoue, Asao B. 2015. *Antiracist Writing Assessment Ecologies: Teaching and
Assessing Writing for a Socially Just Future.* Fort Collins, CO: The
WAC Clearinghouse.

Jacobs, Alan. 2017. *How to Think: A Survival Guide for a World at Odds.*
New York: Currency.

Johnson, David W., Roger T. Johnson, and Karl A. Smith. 2014. "Cooperative Learning: Improving University Instruction by Basing Practice
on Validated Theory." *Journal on Excellence in College Teaching*
25 (3/4): 85–118.

Jones, Francis, and Sara Harris. 2012. "Benefits and Drawbacks of Using
Multiple Instructors to Teach Single Courses." *College Teaching*
60 (4): 132–39.

Kanter, Rosabeth Moss. 1994. "Collaborative Advantage: The Art of
Alliances." *Harvard Business Review* 72 (4): 96–108.

Kauffman Panel on Entrepreneurship in Higher Education. 2008. "Entrepreneurship in American Higher Education." Kansas City, MO: Kauffman
Foundation. https://www.kauffman.org/-/media/kauffman_org
/research-reports-and-covers/2008/07/entrep_high_ed_report.pdf.

Kecskes, Kevin, Seanna Kerrigan, and Judy Patton. 2006. "The Heart of the Matter: Aligning Curriculum, Pedagogy and Engagement in Higher Education." *Metropolitan Universities* 17 (1): 51–61.

Kegan, Robert. 1982. *The Evolving Self*. Cambridge, MA: Harvard University Press.

Kellogg Commission on the Future of State and Land-Grant Universities. 1999. "Returning to Our Roots: The Engaged Institution." Washington, DC: National Association of State Universities and Land Grant Colleges. https://www.aplu.org/library/returning-to-our-roots-the -engaged-institution.

Kerrigan, Seanna M. 2015. "Sustaining Change: Successes, Challenges, and Lessons Learned from Twenty Years of Empowering Students through Community-Based Learning Capstones." *Metropolitan Universities* 26 (3): 11–31.

Kezar, Adrianna J. 2005. "Redesigning for Collaboration within Higher Education: An Exploration into the Developmental Process." *Research in Higher Education* 47 (7): 831–60.

Kezar, Adrianna J., and Jaime Lester. 2009. *Organizing Higher Education for Collaboration: A Guide for Campus Leaders*. San Francisco: Jossey-Bass (Wiley).

King, Joyce E. 1991. "Dysconscious Racism, Ideology, Identity, and the Miseducation of Teachers." *Journal of Negro Education* 60 (2): 133–46.

Kiyama, Judy Marquez, Samuel D. Museus, and Blanca Vega. 2015. "Cultivating Campus Environments to Maximize Success among Latino and Latina College Students." *New Directions for Higher Education* 172 (December): 29–38.

Klein, Ezra. 2020. *Why We're Polarized*. New York: Avid Reader Press.

Kluger, Avraham N., and Angelo DeNisi. 1996. "The Effects of Feedback Interventions on Performance: A Historical Review, a Meta-Analysis, and a Preliminary Feedback Intervention Theory." *Psychological Bulletin* 119 (2): 254–84.

Kohlberg, Lawrence. 1976. "Moral Stages and Moralization: The Cognitive-Developmental Approach." In *Moral Development and Behavior: Theory, Research, and Social Issues*, edited by Thomas Lickona, 31–53. New York: Holt Press.

Krajcik, Joseph S., Phyllis C. Blumenfeld, Ronald W. Marx, and Elliot Soloway. 1994. "A Collaborative Model for Helping Middle Grade

Science Teachers Learn Project-Based Instruction." *Elementary School Journal* 94 (5): 483–97.

Kuh, George D., John H. Schuh, and Elizabeth J. Whitt. 1991. *Involving Colleges: Successful Approaches to Fostering Student Learning and Development Outside the Classroom*. San Francisco: Jossey-Bass.

Labaree, David F. 1997. *How to Succeed in School without Really Learning: The Credentials Race in American Education*. New Haven, CT.: Yale University Press.

Laden, Berta Vigil. 2004. "Serving Emerging Majority Students." *New Directions for Community Colleges* 2004 (127): 5–19.

Ladson-Billings, Gloria. 2014. "Culturally Relevant Pedagogy 2.0: A.k.a. the Remix." *Harvard Educational Review* 84 (1): 74–84.

Ladson-Billings, Gloria, 1947–1995. "Toward a Theory of Culturally Relevant Pedagogy." *American Educational Research Journal* 32: 465–91.

Lave, Jean, and Etienne Wenger. 1991. *Situated Learning: Legitimate Peripheral Participation*. New York: Cambridge University Press.

Levin, John S., and Aida Aliyeva. 2015. "Embedded Neoliberalism within Faculty Behaviors." *Review of Higher Education* 38 (4): 537–63.

Levine, Arthur. 1980. *When Dreams and Heroes Died: A Portrait of Today's College Student*. San Francisco: Jossey-Bass.

Lock, Jennifer, Jacqueline Rainsbury, Tracey Clancy, Patricia Rosenau, and Carla Ferreira. 2018. "Influence of Co-Teaching on Undergraduate Student Learning: A Mixed-Methods Study in Nursing." *Teaching & Learning Inquiry* 6 (1): 38–51.

Lopatto, David. 2003. "The Essential Features of Undergraduate Research." *CUR Quarterly* 24: 139–42.

Markus, Hazel Rose, and Shinobu Kitayama. 1991. "Culture and the Self: Implications for Cognition, Emotion, and Motivation." *Psychological Review* 98 (2): 224–53.

Marx, Ronald W., Phyllis C. Blumenfeld, Joseph S. Krajcik, and Elliot Soloway. 1997. "Enacting Project-Based Science." *Elementary School Journal* 97 (4): 341–58.

McGarr, Olliver, and Amanda Clifford. 2013. "'Just Enough to Make You Take It Seriously': Exploring Students' Attitudes towards Peer Assessment." *Higher Education* 65 (6): 677–93.

McPherson, Miller, Lynn Smith-Lovin, and James M. Cook. 2013. "Birds of a Feather: Homophily in Social Networks." *Annual Review of Sociology* 27 (1): 415–44.

Meisel, Wayne. 2013. "Foreword: Reflecting on Bonner's Journey." In *Deepening Community Engagement in Higher Education: Forging New Pathways*, edited by Ariane Hoy and Mathew Johnson, xi–xiv. New York: Palgrave Macmillan.

Merriënboer, Jeroen J. G. van, and Paul A. Kirschner. 2013. *Ten Steps to Complex Learning: A Systematic Approach to Four-Component Instructional Design*. 2nd ed. New York: Routledge.

Meyer, John W., Francisco O. Ramirez, David John Frank, and Evan Schofer. 2007. "Higher Education as an Institution." In *Sociology of Higher Education: Contributions and Their Contexts*, edited by Patricia J. Gumport, 187–221. Baltimore, MD: Johns Hopkins University Press.

Morelock, John R., Marlena McGlothlin Lester, Michelle D. Klopfer, Alex M. Jardon, Ricky D. Mullins, Erika L. Nicholas, and Ahmed S. Alfaydi. 2017. "Power, Perceptions, and Relationships: A Model of Co-Teaching in Higher Education." *College Teaching* 65 (4): 182–91.

Morin, Rich, Anna Brown, and Rick Fry. 2014. "The Rising Cost of 'Not' Going to College." Web. Washington, DC: Pew Research Center. http://www.pewsocialtrends.org/2014/02/11/the-rising-cost-of-not-going-to-college/.

Moskovitz, Cary. 2017. "Volunteer Expert Readers: Drawing on the University Community to Provide Professional Feedback for Engineering Student Writers." *Advances in Engineering Education* 6 (1). https://advances.asee.org/wp-content/uploads/vol06/issue01/Papers/AEE-20-Moskovitz.pdf.

Moursund, David. 1999. *Project-Based Learning Using Information Technology*. Eugene, OR: International Society for Technology Education.

Museus, Samuel D. 2011. "Generating Ethnic Minority Student Success (GEMS): A Qualitative Analysis of High-Performing Institutions." *Journal of Diversity in Higher Education* 4 (3): 147–62.

———. 2014. "The Culturally Engaging Campus Environments (CECE) Model: A New Theory of College Success among Racially Diverse Student Populations." In *Higher Education: Handbook of Theory and Research*, edited by Michael B. Paulsen, 189–227. New York: Springer.

Museus, Samuel D., and Joanna N. Ravello. 2010. "Characteristics of Academic Advising That Contribute to Racial and Ethnic Minority Student Success at Predominantly White Institutions." *NACADA Journal* 30 (1): 47–58.

Myers, Carrie B., and Scott M. Myers. 2015. "The Use of Learner-Centered Assessment Practices in the United States: The Influence of Individual and Institutional Contexts." *Studies in Higher Education* 40 (10): 1904–18.

Nash, Robert J. 2009. "Crossover Pedagogy: The Collaborative Search for Meaning." *About Campus* 14 (1): 2–9.

National Research Council. 2012. *Education for Life and Work: Developing Transferable Knowledge and Skills in the 21st Century*. Washington, DC: National Academies Press.

National Survey of Student Engagement. 2014. "From Benchmarks to Engagement Indicators and High-Impact Practices." Indianapolis, IN: National Survey of Student Engagement. http://nsse.indiana .edu/pdf/Benchmarks%20to%20Indicators.pdf.

National Task Force on Civic Learning and Democratic Engagement. 2012. "A Crucible Moment: College Learning and Democracy's Future." Washington, DC: Association of American Colleges and Universities. https://www.aacu.org/sites/default/files/files/crucible /Crucible_508F.pdf.

Nelson, Adam R. 2001. *Education and Democracy: The Meaning of Alexander Meiklejohn, 1872–1964*. Madison: University of Wisconsin Press.

Newman, Frank. 1985. "Higher Education and the American Resurgence." Princeton, NJ: Carnegie Foundation for the Advancement of Teaching.

Norman, Don. 2013. *The Design of Everyday Things*. Revised and Expanded. New York: Basic Books.

Nuñez, Anne-Marie. 2009. "Latino Students' Transitions to College: A Social and Intercultural Capital Perspective." *Harvard Educational Review* 79 (1): 22–48.

Oliveri, María Elena, René Lawless, and Hillary Molloy. 2017. "A Literature Review on Collaborative Problem Solving for College and Workforce Readiness." RR-17-06. Princeton, NJ: GRE-ETS.

Orrell, Janice. 2006. "Feedback on Learning Achievement: Rhetoric and Reality." *Teaching in Higher Education* 11 (4): 441–56.

Paris, Django. 2009. "'They're in My Culture, They Speak the Same Way': African American Language in Multiethnic High Schools." *Harvard Educational Review* 79: 428–47.

———. 2011. *Language across Difference: Ethnicity, Communication, and Youth Identities in Changing Urban Schools*. Cambridge: Cambridge University Press.

————. 2012. "Culturally Sustaining Pedagogy: A Needed Change in Stance, Terminology, and Practice." *Educational Researcher* 41 (3): 93–97.

Paris, Django, and H. Samy Alim. 2014. "What Are We Seeking to Sustain through Culturally Sustaining Pedagogy? A Loving Critique Forward." *Harvard Educational Review* 84 (1): 85–100.

Pascarella, Ernest T., and Patrick T. Terenzini. 2005. *How College Affects Students: A Third Decade of Research*. San Francisco: Jossey-Bass.

Perera, Jennifer, Nagarajah Lee, Khin Win, Joachim Perera, and Lionel Wijesuriya. 2008. "Formative Feedback to Students: The Mismatch between Faculty Perceptions and Student Expectations." *Medical Teacher* 30 (4): 395–99.

Pizzolato, Jane Elizabeth, Kim Nguyen Tu-Lien, Marc Johnston, and Sherry Wang. 2012. "Understanding Context: Cultural, Relational, & Psychological Interactions in Self-Authorship Development." *Journal of College Student Development* 53 (5): 656–79.

Prince, Michael. 2004. "Does Active Learning Work? A Review of the Research." *Journal of Engineering Education* 93 (3): 223–31.

Putnam, Robert D. 2000. *Bowling Alone: The Collapse and Revival of American Community*. New York: Simon & Schuster.

Pyawasay, Sasanehsaeh. 2017. "Walking in Two Worlds: Education Institutions as Modern-Day Boarding Schools." Paper presentation presented at the University Council of Education Administration Convention 2017, Denver, CO, November 16. http://www.ucea.org/wp-content/uploads/2017/09/UCEA2017ProgramDRAFTSept28.pdf.

Ramaley, Judith A. 2001. "Why Do We Engage in Engagement?" *Metropolitan Universities: An International Forum* 12 (3): 13–19.

Reinholz, Daniel L. 2016. "The Assessment Cycle: A Model for Learning through Peer Assessment." *Assessment & Evaluation in Higher Education* 41 (2): 301–15.

————. 2018. "Peer Feedback for Learning Mathematics." *American Mathematical Monthly* 125 (7): 653–58.

Reitenauer, Vicki L., Katherine Elaine Draper-Beard, and Noah Schultz. 2018. "Metamorphosis Inside and Out: Transformative Learning at Portland State University." *Metropolitan Universities* 29 (3): 43–52.

Rendón, Laura I., Romero E. Jalomo, and Amaury Nora. 2000. "Theoretical Considerations in the Study of Minority Student Retention in Higher

Education." In *Reworking the Student Departure Puzzle*, edited by John M. Braxton, 125–156. Nashville, TN: Vanderbilt University Press.

Rhoades, Gary. 2014. "The Higher Education We Choose, Collectively: Reembodying and Repoliticizing Choice." *Journal of Higher Education* 85 (6): 917–30.

Rittel, Horst W. J., and Melvin M. Webber. 1973. "Dilemmas in a General Theory of Planning." *Policy Sciences* 4: 155–69.

Robinson, Marilynne. 2016. "Save Our Public Universities." *Harper's Magazine*, March 2016.

Rosenbaum, James E. 2001. *Beyond College for All: Career Paths for the Forgotten Half*. New York: Russell Sage Foundation.

Ryan, Richard M., and Edward L. Deci. 2000. "Self-Determination Theory and the Facilitation of Intrinsic Motivation, Social Development, and Well-Being." *American Psychologist* 55 (1): 68–78.

Saltmarsh, John, Matthew Hartley, and Patti Clayton. 2009. "Democratic Engagement White Paper." Boston: New England Resource Center for Higher Education. https://scholarworks.umb.edu/nerche_pubs/45/.

Schein, Edgar H. 2013. *Humble Inquiry: The Gentle Art of Asking Instead of Telling*. Oakland, CA: Berrett-Koehler.

Schön, Donald A. 1983. *The Reflective Practitioner: How Professionals Think in Action*. New York: Basic Books.

Schultz, P. Wesley, Paul R. Hernandez, Anna Woodcock, Mica Estrada, Randie C. Chance, Maria Aguilar, and Richard T. Serpe. 2011. "Patching the Pipeline Reducing Educational Disparities in the Sciences through Minority Training Programs." *Educational Evaluation and Policy Analysis* 33: 95–114.

Senge, Peter M. 1990. *The Fifth Discipline: The Art & Practice of the Learning Organization*. New York: Doubleday.

Shute, Valerie J. 2008. "Focus on Formative Feedback." *Review of Educational Research* 78 (1): 153–89.

Smith, Barbara Leigh, Jean MacGregor, Roberta S. Matthews, and Faith Gabelnick. 2004. *Learning Communities: Reforming Undergraduate Education*. San Francisco: Jossey-Bass.

Solórzano, Daniel G., and Tara J. Yosso. 2002. "Critical Race Methodology: Counter-Storytelling as an Analytical Framework for Education Research." *Qualitative Inquiry* 8 (1): 23.

Sommers, Nancy. 2006. "Across the Drafts." *College Composition & Communication* 58 (2): 248–57.

Spencer-Oatey, Helen. 2013. "Maximizing the Benefits of International Education Collaborations: Managing Interaction Processes." *Journal of Studies in International Education* 17 (3): 244–61.

Springer, Leonard, Mary Elizabeth Stanne, and Samuel S. Donovan. 1999. "Effects of Small-Group Learning on Undergraduates in Science, Mathematics, Engineering, and Technology: A Meta-Analysis." *Review of Educational Research* 69 (1): 21–51.

Steele, Claude M. 2011. *Whistling Vivaldi: How Stereotypes Affect Us.* New York: W. W. Norton.

Stephens, Nicole M., Stephanie A. Fryberg, Hazel Rose Markus, Camille S. Johnson, and Rebecca Covarrubias. 2012. "Unseen Disadvantage: How American Universities' Focus on Independence Undermines the Academic Performance of First-Generation College Students." *Journal of Personality and Social Psychology* 102 (6): 1178–97.

Stiggins, Richard J. 2002. "Assessment Crisis: The Absence of Assessment *for* Learning." *Phi Delta Kappan* 83 (10): 758.

Strayhorn, Terrell L., and Joan B. Hirt. 2008. "Student Engagement and Student Success at Historically Black and Hispanic-Serving Institutions." In *Understanding Minority-Serving Institutions,* edited by Marybeth Gasman, B. Baez, and C. S. V. Turner, 203–16. Albany: State University of New York Press.

Sun, Zhong, Chin-Hsi Lin, Minhua Wu, Jianshe Zhou, and Liming Luo. 2018. "A Tale of Two Communication Tools: Discussion-forum and Mobile Instant-messaging Apps in Collaborative Learning." *British Journal of Educational Technology* 49 (2): 248–61.

Taczak, Kara, and Liane Robertson. 2016. "Reiterative Reflection in the Twenty-First-Century Writing Classroom: An Integrated Approach to Teaching for Transfer." In *A Rhetoric of Reflection,* edited by Kathleen Blake Yancey, 42–63. Logan: Utah State University Press.

Talloires Network. 2005. "The Talloires Declaration on the Civic Roles and Social Responsibilities of Higher Education." https://talloires network.tufts.edu/wp-content/uploads/TalloiresDeclaration 2005.pdf.

Tanaka, Greg. 2003. *The Intercultural Campus: Transcending Culture & Power in American Higher Education.* New York: P. Lang.

Thelin, John R. 2019. *A History of American Higher Education.* 3rd ed. Baltimore, MD: Johns Hopkins University Press.

Thomas, John W. 2000. "A Review of Research on Project-Based Learning." San Rafael, CA: The Autodesk Foundation. http://www.bie.org/research/study/review_of_project_based_learning_2000.

Tierney, William G. 1992. "An Anthropological Analysis of Student Participation in College." *Journal of Higher Education* 63 (6): 603–18.

———. 1999. "Models of Minority College-Going and Retention: Cultural Integrity versus Cultural Suicide." *Journal of Negro Education* 68 (1): 80.

Tinto, Vincent. 1993. *Leaving College: Rethinking the Causes and Cures of Student Attrition.* Chicago: University of Chicago Press.

———. 2005. *College Student Retention: Formula for Student Success.* Santa Barbara, CA: Greenwood Publishing Group.

Tisdell, Elizabeth J., and Mary-Jane Eisen. 2000. "Team Teaching and Learning in Adult Education: From Negotiating Relationships to Implementing Learning Alternatives." *New Directions for Adult & Continuing Education*, no. 87: 83–89.

Tobin, Thomas J., and Kirsten T. Behling. 2018. *Reach Everyone, Teach Everyone: Universal Design for Learning in Higher Education.* Morgantown: West Virginia University Press.

Torrance, Wendy E. F. 2013. "Entrepreneurial Campuses: Action, Impact, and Lessons Learned from the Kauffman Campus Initiative." Kansas City, MO: Ewing Marion Kauffman Foundation. https://www.kauffman.org/-/media/kauffman_org/research-reports-and-covers/2013/08/entrepreneurialcampusesessay.pdf.

Torres, Vasti. 2006. "A Mixed Method Study Testing Data-Model Fit of a Retention Model for Latino/a Students at Urban Universities." *Journal of College Student Development* 47 (3): 299–318.

Trilling, Bernie, and Charles Fadel. 2009. *21st Century Skills: Learning for Life in Our Times.* San Francisco: Jossey-Bass.

Trimbur, John. 1989. "Consensus and Difference in Collaborative Learning." *College English* 51 (October): 602–16.

Trow, Martin. 1970. "Reflections on the Transition from Mass to Universal Higher Education." *Daedalus* 99 (1): 1–42.

US Department of Education. 2006. "A Test of Leadership: Charting the Future of U.S. Higher Education." Washington, DC: US Department of Education.

———. 2017. "Status and Trends in Education of Racial and Ethnic Groups." NCES Publication No. 2017-051. Washington, DC: US

Department of Education. https://nces.ed.gov/programs/raceindi
cators/indicator rbb.asp.

Vygotsky, Lev. 1962. *Thought and Language*. Cambridge, MA: MIT Press.

Weaver, Gabriela C., Cianan B. Russell, and Donald J. Wink. 2008.
"Inquiry-Based and Research-Based Laboratory Pedagogies in
Undergraduate Science." *Nature Chemical Biology* 4: 577–80.

Wolf, Lorraine W. 2018. "Undergraduate Research as Engaged Student
Learning." *New Directions for Teaching & Learning* 154: 75–85.

Wolf Shenk, Joshua. 2014. "The End of 'Genius.'" *New York Times*, July 20,
2014

Womak, Anne-Marie. 2017. "Teaching Is Accommodation: Universally
Designing Composition Classrooms and Syllabi." *College Composition &
Communication* 68 (3): 494–525.

Yancey, Kathleen Blake, ed. 2016. *A Rhetoric of Reflection*. Logan: Utah
State University Press.

Yancey, Kathleen Blake, Liane Robertson, and Kara Taczak. 2014. *Writing
across Contexts: Transfer, Composition, and Sites of Writing*. Logan:
Utah State University Press.

Young, Vershawn Ashanti. 2009. "'Nah, We Straight': An Argument
against Code Switching." *JAC: A Journal of Rhetoric, Culture & Politics*
29 (1/2): 49–76.

Zemsky, Robert M. 2009. *Making Reform Work: The Case for Transforming
American Higher Education*. New Brunswick, NJ: Rutgers University
Press.

INDEX

access to higher education, 82, 152
accountability, 33–34, 139, 170
active learning, 19, 29–30
advisors/advising, 44, 53, 57, 65, 67, 76, 81–82, 83; cluster, 164; in culturally engaged colleges, 85–88, 91, 92; intrusive, 67; peer-based, 75, 76; as support service, 84, 91, 94
agency of students, 23, 43, 147–48
Aliyeva, Aida, 20
American Indian Science and Engineering Society, 67–68
Americans with Disabilities Act, 17
anchor institutions, 153, 162
Antioch University, 77
antiracist assessment ecology, 121–23
antiracist policies, programs, and practices, 46–47, 196, 200
apprenticeships, 90–91
Aristocracy of Everyone: The Politics of Education and the Future (Barber), 16
Arizona State University, 174–80
Asian American Native American Pacific Islander Institutions, 1, 186–87
Asian American and Pacific Islander students, 27, 154–55

assimilation, 43, 70, 186, 193–94
Association of American Colleges and Universities (AAC&U), 30, 36, 159–60; Value Rubric for Teamwork, 36

backwards design, 143, 183–84
Ball, Arnetha, 54
Barr, Robert, 94
Beloit College, 90–92; Liberal Arts Practice Center, 90–91; Sanger Summer Research Program, 91
belonging, sense of, 60–61
Bernstine, Daniel, 161–62
blended learning, 19
Blum, Susan D., 93–94
Bonner AmeriCorps Program, 161
Bonner Foundation, 156–57, 160, 167
Bonner Pipeline Project, 167
Bonner Program, 156–62, 165–66; Freshman and Sophomore Inquiry programs, 163–64
Boyer, Ernest, 152, 155
Boyer Commission on Educating Undergraduates in the Research University, 28, 29, 89, 94, 136–37
bridge programs, 7

justification, 21; shortcomings, 21–27
individual liberty, 19
innovation, 55, 169. *See also* entrepreneurship
Inoue, Asao, 48, 121–22, 196
inquiry, shared agenda for, 32–33
inquiry-driven learning, 28–29
inquiry problems, 130
institutional culture, 13, 32; collaborative learner identity, 61–65; cultural congruity, 69–72; definition, 50; individual achievement as focus, 50–51; interdependence and collaboration in, 56–61; network programs with local communities, 13, 66–69; reframing undergraduate education and, 52–61
institutional transformation, 40–49, 184–85; co-teaching and, 82; in entrepreneurial institutions, 172–73, 174
interdependence, 9, 10, 22, 26, 38, 41, 45, 52, 61, 70–71; feedback and, 104; in hubs, 75; as institutional culture component, 56–61; in STEM programs, 57–58
interdisciplinary approach, 76, 144, 145, 156; in community-engaged learning, 162, 163–64, 166; entrepreneurial, 174, 175; in student research programs, 91, 137
internships, 41–42, 62, 63, 66, 67, 68, 131, 137, 144, 149; in first-year curriculum, 169–70; in research, 89, 91

Jacobs, Alan, 36
job preparation system, higher education as, 17–18, 20

Kauffman Campuses Initiative, 173, 174–80
Kauffman Panel on Entrepreneurship in Higher Education, 173–74

Kezar, Adrianna, 41
Kilpatrick, William, 128
Kirscher, Paul, 134
knowledge: acquisition, 136, 139; co-construction, 31

Labaree, David, 20
Ladson-Billings, Gloria, 185
La Sierra University, 119
Latinx students, 60, 87, 187–88
leadership: servant, 62–63; transformational, 52
learning communities, 7, 76, 77–78, 98
learning management systems, 94, 118–19, 197
learning reward cycle, 123
Lee, Linda, 196
Lester, Jaime, 41
Levin, Joel, 20
liberal arts, 15, 18, 34–35, 90–91, 140, 175
licensure examinations, 19
listening skills, 32–33, 78, 80, 182
local problem-solving-based curriculum, 135–51, 184, 187–88; academic statements, 140–42, 143; case examples, 137–52; community-engaged, 151–68; engineering education, 137–39, 142, 143–44; entrepreneurial, 178, 179; network programs, 66–69, 146, 147; at TCUs, 144–51

mainstream culture and practices, in higher education, 19–21, 196; adverse social effects, 197–98. *See also* Predominantly White Institutions (PWIs)
market value, 179–81
mathematics education: innovative approach, 170; local problem-solving approach, 130–31; remedial, 2, 119, 130, 145
math emporia, 7, 114
Meiklejohn, Alexander, 18

support services, 82–88, 94, 148, 151, 169; culturally engaging, 84–88

sustainability, 139, 163, 164

Tagg, John, 94

teaching, collaborative learning-based redesign, 44–45

Teaching for Transfer (TFT) curriculum, 116–17

Teaming: How Organizations Learn, Innovate, and Compete in the Global Economy (Edmondson), 22–23

teamwork, 32–23, 34, 35, 36, 94, 129

Tisdell, Elizabeth J., 79, 80

Title IX, 17

Tribal Colleges and Universities (TCUs), 1, 9, 119–20, 186–87, 195–96, 200–201; local problem-solving-based curriculum, 144–51. *See also names of individual colleges*

triple bottom line, 180–81

tutoring centers, 76

tutors/tutoring, 7, 83, 145, 149

21st Century Skills: Learning for Life in Our Times (Trilling and Fadel), 30

undergraduate education models, 16–17, 20

underrepresented students: cultural and ethnic identities, 47; equitable spaces for, 47–48; shared problem-solving cultures, 38; support programs and services, 73–75, 83

US Constitution, 39

US Department of Education, College Scorecard, 18

US Department of Justice, 191

Universal Design (UD), 42–43, 200

University Innovation Fellows, 177

University of Arizona, Collaborative Learning Spaces, 112–13

University of Calgary, 78

University of Delaware, 137

University of Michigan, 78

University of Montana, 131

University of Pennsylvania, 1

University of Vermont, 77

University of Wisconsin–Madison, 1, 9, 190; Experimental College, 18; Integrated Liberal Arts program, 18

urban universities, community-engaged learning program, 156, 161–66

utilitarian-vocational model, of undergraduate education, 16, 17, 20

value, 179–81, 183

ventures, 174, 177–78, 185

Volunteer Expert Reader (VER) approach, 105–7, 111

volunteering, 153, 157–58

Wake Forest University, 174–80

Wiewel, Wim, 162

Williams, Raymond, 197

Worcester Polytechnic Institute, 137

writing coursework, 122–23

Yale Report of 1828, 15–16

Yancey, Kathleen Blake, 116, 118

York College, 137

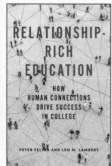
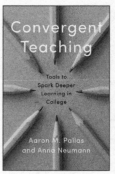
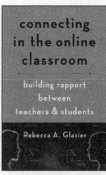